Good Housekeeping

ONE-POT COOKING

Good Housekeeping

ONE-POT COOKING

over 100 brilliant recipes – all cooked in one pot

COLLINS & BROWN

First published in hardback in Great Britain in 2003
First published in paperback in Great Britain in 2004
by Collins & Brown Limited
The Chrysalis Building
London W10 6SP

An imprint of **Chrysalis** Books Group plc

Published in association with The National Magazine Company Limited.
Good Housekeeping is a trade mark of The National Magazine Company Limited.

The Good Housekeeping website address is www.goodhousekeeping.co.uk

1 2 3 4 5 6 7 8 9 0

British Library Cataloguing-in-Publication Data:
A catalogue record for this book is available from the British Library.

ISBN 1 84340 209 2

Front jacket photograph: Steve Baxter
Back jacket photograph: Phillip Webb
Spine photograph: Steve Baxter

Photographers: Marie-Louise Avery pages 51, 52, 108, 112, 123; Steve Baxter pages 16,
30, 45, 46, 49, 65, 69, 111, 132; Martin Brigdale page 138; Peter Cassidy pages 15,
33; Jean Cazals pages 63, 103, 105, 115, 117; Laurie Evans pages 11, 25, 59, 97, 133;
Graham Kirk pages 81, 91, 135; William Lingwood pages 87, 93, 124; Michael Paul
page 39; Roger Stowell page 35; Martin Thompson pages 21, 29, 55, 73, 74; Philip
Webb pages 41, 98, 131, 141; Elizabeth Zeschin pages 77, 81, 85, 101, 118, 119.

Photographs: page 2 Stir-fried prawns and noodles in yellow bean sauce (see page 42);
page 5 Wild mushroom sauté (see page 116); page 6 Caribbean chicken (see page 31)

Reproduction by Classicscan Pte Ltd, Singapore
Printed and bound in Malaysia by Times Offset Printing
This book was typeset using Futura and Joanna

CONTENTS

INTRODUCTION

I'm a great believer in making things as simple as possible – why use three pans when you can create a dish in one? However much I enjoy cooking, I find the most boring part is the washing up. Even if you've a dishwasher, it's still a drag. So in this book, not only have we compiled a selection of incredibly tasty recipes that are triple-tested to guarantee success, we've reduced the number of bowls and pots you use in their preparation – so you ultimately will have only one pot to wash.

I recommend you invest in one really good quality, large, heavy-based flameproof casserole with a tightly fitting lid – something that can be used on the hob and in the oven (so it mustn't have plastic or wooden handles). Buy the most expensive one you can afford – it will guarantee that the food cooks evenly, doesn't stick to the base and, above all, will ensure the best possible result. Stainless steel, enamel cast iron or anodised aluminium are all good choices and will save you scrubbing time at the sink.

Occasionally a recipe may indicate that you need to use a baking sheet or grill pan as well as a pot. Again, invest in a good quality heavy one, such as anodised aluminium and top it with a non-stick sheet, such as Bake-O-Glide or Teflon. Nothing sticks to it, so rinse it after use and use again and again for stress-free cooking and clearing away.

If you don't know where to start given such a scrumptious selection of ideas, may I recommend my two favourites – Caribbean chicken (a weekly meal in our family), shown left and on page 31, and zabaglione, on page 129.

Happy cooking.

Felicity

FELICITY BARNUM-BOBB

COOKERY EDITOR

1

SOUPS

SUMMER VEGETABLE SOUP WITH HERB PISTOU

SQUASH AND SWEET POTATO SOUP

CHEESY LEEK SOUP

MINESTRONE ALLA MILANESE

THAI CHICKEN BROTH

SCOTCH BROTH

SPICED BEEF AND NOODLE SOUP

CLAM CHOWDER

SMOKED COD AND SWEETCORN CHOWDER

MEDITERRANEAN FISH SOUP WITH ROUILLE

MISO MUSHROOM AND SPINACH SOUP

BOUILLABAISSE

Summer vegetable soup with herb pistou

PREPARATION TIME: 45 minutes
COOKING TIME: 1 hour
PER SERVING: 291cals, 64g fat, 38g carbohydrate

SERVES 6

3tbsp sunflower oil
1 medium onion, finely chopped
225g (8oz) waxy potatoes, finely diced
175g (6oz) carrots, finely diced
1 medium turnip, finely diced
4 bay leaves
6 large sage leaves
2 courgettes – around 375g (13oz) – finely diced
175g (6oz) French beans, trimmed and halved
125g (4oz) shelled small peas
225g (8oz) tomatoes, deseeded and finely diced
1 small head broccoli, broken into florets
Herb Pistou (see below) or ready-made pesto to serve

Pistou is the French equivalent of the Italian pesto and it adds a Mediterranean touch to this tasty summer soup.

1 Heat the oil in a large pan, add the onion, potatoes, carrots and turnip and fry over a gentle heat for 10 minutes. Add 1.7 litres (3 pints) of cold water, season well with salt and freshly ground black pepper, bring to the boil and add the bay and sage leaves. Simmer for 25 minutes.

2 Add the courgettes, French beans, peas and the tomatoes. Return to the boil and simmer for 10–15 minutes. Add the broccoli 5 minutes before the end of the cooking time.

3 Remove the bay and sage leaves and adjust the seasoning. Pour the soup into bowls, remove 12 French beans, add a spoonful of Herb Pistou or pesto and garnish with the reserved French beans.

TO PREPARE AHEAD Make the Herb Pistou up to one week ahead, put into a sealable jar, cover and chill. The day before, complete the recipe to the end of step 1, cool, cover and chill. Cut up the other vegetables and store them in a polythene bag in the fridge.
TO USE Complete the recipe.

Herb pistou

¾ level tsp sea salt
6 garlic cloves, chopped
15g (½oz) chopped fresh basil
12tbsp olive oil

1 Using a pestle and mortar or a strong bowl and the end of a rolling pin, or a mini processor, pound together the salt and garlic until smooth.

2 Add the basil and pound down to a paste then blend in the olive oil, a little at a time.

Squash and sweet potato soup

PREPARATION TIME: 20 minutes
COOKING TIME: 35 minutes
PER SERVING: 100cals, 2g fat, 19g carbohydrate

SERVES 8

1 tbsp olive oil
1 large onion, finely chopped
2 medium red chillies, deseeded and chopped
2 level tsp coriander seeds, crushed
1 butternut squash – around 750g (1lb 10oz) – peeled
    and roughly chopped
2 medium sweet potatoes, peeled and roughly chopped
2 medium tomatoes, skinned and diced
1.7 litres (3 pints) hot vegetable stock

Butternut squash has a deep orange flesh, and its slightly sweet flavour combines well with the sweet potatoes in this spicy soup.

1 Heat the oil in a large pan and fry the onion until soft – around 10 minutes. Add the chilli and coriander seeds to the pan and cook for 1–2 minutes.
2 Add the squash, potatoes and tomatoes and cook for 5 minutes, then add the hot stock, cover and bring to the boil. Simmer gently for 15 minutes or until the vegetables are soft.
3 Using a stick blender, whiz the soup in the pan until smooth. Reheat to serve.

TO FREEZE Complete the recipe to the end of step 3. Cool and put in a freezerproof container. Seal and freeze for up to three months.
TO USE Thaw for 4 hours at cool room temperature. Put in a pan and bring to the boil. Simmer for 10 minutes or until hot right through.

Cheesy leek soup

PREPARATION TIME: 15 minutes
COOKING TIME: 40 minutes
PER SERVING: 380cals, 32g fat, 9g carbohydrate

SERVES 6

50g (2oz) butter
1 large onion – about 225g/8oz – finely chopped
700g (1½lb) trimmed leeks, roughly chopped
1 level tbsp plain flour
1.4 litres (2½ pints) chicken or turkey stock
142ml carton double cream
2 level tsp grainy mustard
225g (8oz) Stilton or Gruyère cheese, diced
Shavings of Stilton to garnish

This hearty soup can be made in minutes, and is a good way to use up any leftover hard cheese.

1 Melt the butter in a large pan, add the onion and cook for 5 minutes or until soft. Add the leeks and cook for 15 minutes, stirring from time to time.
2 Add the flour and mix until smooth, stirring continuously, then add the stock. Bring to the boil and simmer gently for 15 minutes.
3 Reduce the heat until the soup is bubbling gently, then stir in the cream and mustard. Add the cheese in batches, allowing it to melt between each addition. Season well with salt and freshly ground black pepper and serve in warmed soup bowls, garnished with the Stilton.

TO PREPARE AHEAD Complete the recipe. Cool the soup quickly, cover and chill.
TO USE Warm the soup through gently in a pan.

Minestrone alla Milanese

PREPARATION TIME: 40 minutes
COOKING TIME: 1 hour 20 minutes
PER SERVING: 320cals, 19g fat, 25g carbohydrate

SERVES 6

50g (2oz) butter

125g (4oz) pancetta or streaky bacon, cut into small dice

450g (1lb) onions, cut into small dice

175g (6oz) carrots, cut into small dice

175g (6oz) swede or turnip, cut into small dice

125g (4oz) celery, cut into small dice

125g (4oz) courgettes, cut into small dice

75g (3oz) French beans, finely chopped

175g (6oz) potatoes, sliced

75g (3oz) Savoy cabbage, finely shredded

1.7 litres (3 pints) beef stock

Parmesan rind (optional)

396g can chopped tomatoes

396g can cannellini or borlotti beans, drained and rinsed

50g (2oz) freshly grated Parmesan cheese

Each region of Italy has its own version of minestrone in which local produce is highlighted. The Milanese version is believed to be the original, using the region's wonderful butter and vegetables from its fertile plains. You can add almost any vegetable to a minestrone, but you must have onions, celery, carrots, beans, potatoes and tomatoes. Normally it is cooked for about 3 hours, but this version is cooked for 1 hour only; make it the day before to allow the flavours to develop.

1 Melt the butter in a large pan. Sauté the pancetta or bacon and onions for 5 minutes or until soft, stirring frequently. Stir in the carrots, swede or turnip and celery and sauté for 5 minutes.

2 Add the courgettes, French beans and potatoes. Cook, stirring, for about 5 minutes or until all the vegetables are coated in butter.

3 Add the Savoy cabbage with the beef stock, Parmesan rind, if using, and chopped tomatoes and season with salt and freshly ground black pepper. Bring to the boil, then cover and simmer for 45 minutes. Add the beans and cook for a further 15 minutes.

4 Stir in half the Parmesan cheese and serve the remainder separately, to be sprinkled over the minestrone to taste.

TO FREEZE Complete the recipe to the end of step 4. Cool and put in a freezerproof container. Seal and freeze for up to 1 month.
TO USE Thaw overnight at cool room temperature. Put in a pan and bring back to the boil. Cover and simmer for 10 minutes. Add the Parmesan before serving.

Thai chicken broth

PREPARATION TIME: 30 minutes
COOKING TIME: 20 minutes
PER SERVING: 210cals, 7g fat, 13g carbohydrate

SERVES 4

1 tbsp olive oil

4 boneless, skinless chicken thighs – around 300g (11oz)
  – cubed

3 garlic cloves, roughly chopped

2 medium red chillies, deseeded and finely diced

1 lemongrass stalk, finely sliced

5cm (2in) piece fresh root ginger, finely chopped

150ml (¼ pint) white wine

1 litre (1¾ pints) chicken stock

8 coriander sprigs

50g (2oz) rice noodles

125g (4oz) French beans, trimmed and halved

125g (4oz) beansprouts

4 spring onions, sliced

2 tbsp Thai fish sauce (nam pla)

Juice of ½ lime

Don't be put off by the long list of ingredients for this soup – speedy cooking makes up for it. Use fine egg noodles in place of rice noodles if you prefer.

1 Heat the oil in a large pan, then add the chicken pieces, garlic, chillies, lemongrass and ginger and cook for 3–5 minutes or until the chicken is opaque.

2 Add the white wine, bring to the boil and simmer until reduced by half. Add the stock, bring to the boil, then simmer for 5 minutes or until the chicken is cooked through.

3 Pick the leaves off the coriander and put them to one side. Finely chop the coriander stalks. Add the noodles to the pan and cook for 1 minute then add the French beans and chopped coriander stalks. Cook for 3 minutes.

4 Add the beansprouts and spring onions along with the fish sauce and lime juice. Bring to the boil and taste for seasoning.

5 Ladle the noodles and broth among four warmed, deep bowls, making sure each serving has its fair share of chicken and beansprouts. Garnish with the coriander leaves and serve immediately.

Scotch broth

PREPARATION TIME: 20 minutes
COOKING TIME: 2 hours
PER SERVING: 150cals, 1g fat, 25g carbohydrate

SERVES 8

1 piece of marrow bone – around 350g (12oz)

1.4kg (3lb) piece of beef skirt – ask your butcher for this

300ml (½ pint) broth mix (to include pearl barley, red lentils, split peas and green peas), soaked according to the instructions on the pack

2 medium carrots, finely chopped

1 medium parsnip, finely chopped

2 medium onions, finely chopped

¼ white cabbage, finely chopped

1 leek, finely chopped

1–2 level tbsp salt

2 level tbsp chopped fresh parsley to serve

This recipe is really two meals in one – a starter and a main course. The beef is cooked to flavour the stock, then removed before serving. Later you divide up the meat and serve it with a potato and turnip mash.

1 Put the marrow bone and beef skirt into a 5.7 litre (10 pint) stock pot and add 2.6 litres (4½ pints) of cold water – there should be enough to cover the meat.

2 Bring the water to the boil, remove the scum from the surface with a spoon and discard. Turn the heat down low, add the broth mix and simmer, partially covered, for 1½ hours, skimming the surface occasionally.

3 Add the carrots, parsnip, onions, cabbage and leek and another 600ml (1 pint) of cold water, cover to bring to the boil quickly, then simmer for 30 minutes.

4 Remove the marrow bone and piece of beef from the broth. Season the broth well with the salt and some freshly ground black pepper, stir in the chopped parsley and serve.

Spiced beef and noodle soup

PREPARATION TIME: 10 minutes
COOKING TIME: 15 minutes
PER SERVING: 190cals, 10g fat, 12g carbohydrate

SERVES 4

2tbsp sunflower oil

225g (8oz) fillet steak, cut into thin strips

1.1 litres (2 pints) beef stock

2–3tbsp Thai fish sauce (nam pla)

1 large red chilli, deseeded and finely chopped

1 lemongrass stalk, trimmed and thinly sliced

2.5cm (1in) piece root ginger, peeled and finely chopped

6 spring onions, halved lengthways and cut into 2.5cm
   (1in) lengths

1 garlic clove, crushed

¼ level tsp caster sugar

15g (½oz) dried porcini or shiitake mushrooms, broken
   into pieces and soaked in 150ml (¼ pint) boiling water
   for 15 minutes

50g (2oz) medium egg noodles

125g (4oz) spinach leaves, well washed and roughly
   chopped

4 level tbsp chopped fresh coriander

This hearty meal in a bowl takes its influence from fragrant Asian flavours. If you can't find lemongrass, add grated lemon rind and juice to taste.

1 Heat the oil in a large pan, then brown the meat in two batches and put to one side.
2 Pour the stock into the pan with 2tbsp of the fish sauce, the chilli, lemongrass, ginger, spring onions, garlic, sugar and the mushrooms and their soaking liquid. Bring the mixture to the boil.
3 Break the noodles up slightly and add them to the pan, then stir gently until they begin to separate. Simmer the soup, stirring occasionally, for 4–5 minutes or until the noodles are just tender.
4 Stir in the spinach, coriander and reserved beef. Season with salt and freshly ground black pepper, adding the remaining fish sauce to taste, then serve the soup in warmed bowls.

Clam chowder

PREPARATION TIME: 40 minutes
COOKING TIME: 45 minutes
PER SERVING: 490cals, 22g fat, 33g carbohydrate

SERVES 8

1.5kg (3¼lb) fresh clams, washed, tapped and any open
   or damaged ones discarded

2tbsp vegetable oil

2 medium onions, chopped

2 medium carrots, chopped

4 sticks celery, sliced diagonally

3 medium potatoes – around 450g (1lb) – such as Maris
   Piper, diced

25g (1oz) plain flour

75ml (3fl oz) bourbon whiskey

284ml carton double cream

1 level tbsp chopped fresh thyme

2 bay leaves

This is a thick, chunky soup. Look out for clams that are tightly shut with no chipped or broken shells.

1 Put the clams in a large pan with 300ml (½ pint) of cold water, cover with a lid and bring to the boil. Steam for 1–2 minutes or until all the shells have opened. Drain, keeping the cooking liquor to one side. Cool the clams a little then remove from their shells, discarding any that don't open. Chill the clams until needed and set aside the shells for use as decoration if you like.

2 Heat the oil in the same pan, add the onions, carrots, celery and potatoes and cook gently for 5 minutes. Stir in the flour and cook for a further 2 minutes.

3 Pour the whiskey into a ladle, hold over a gas flame, ignite with a match and pour over the vegetables. Add the reserved clam cooking liquor, the double cream, thyme and bay leaves. Season with salt and freshly ground black pepper and cook gently for 20 minutes or until the vegetables have softened.

4 Add the clams, then cook for 2–3 minutes to heat them through. Pour into bowls and garnish with the clam shells, if using.

TO FREEZE Complete the recipe to the end of step 3 and remove the bay leaves. Cool and put in a freezerproof container. Put the clams in a separate container and freeze both for up to one month.

TO USE Thaw at cool room temperature for 3–4 hours. Heat the soup in a covered pan until boiling, then simmer for 2–3 minutes. Add the clams and heat through.

Smoked cod and sweetcorn chowder

PREPARATION TIME: 15 minutes
COOKING TIME: 40 minutes
PER SERVING: 530cals, 30g fat, 36g carbohydrate

SERVES 6

130g pack cubed pancetta

50g (2oz) butter

3 leeks – about 450g (1lb) – trimmed and thinly sliced

25g (1oz) plain flour

568ml carton semi-skimmed or full-fat milk

700g (1½lb) undyed smoked cod loin or haddock,
    skinned and cut into 2cm (¾in) cubes

326g can sweetcorn in water, drained

450g (1lb) small new potatoes, sliced

142ml carton double cream

½ level tsp paprika

2tbsp chopped fresh flat-leafed parsley to garnish

Fish, potatoes, pancetta, leeks and sweetcorn combine in a wonderfully creamy broth. Smoked cod loin has a lovely flavour and is a good thick, chunky cut.

1 Fry the pancetta in a large pan, until the fat runs out. Add the butter to the pan to melt, then add the leeks and cook until softened.

2 Stir in the flour and cook for a few seconds, then pour in the milk and 300ml (½ pint) of cold water.

3 Add the fish to the pan with the sweetcorn and potatoes. Bring to the boil and simmer for 10–15 minutes, until the potatoes are cooked.

4 Stir in the cream, season with salt and freshly ground black pepper and the paprika and cook for 2–3 minutes to warm through. Ladle into wide shallow bowls and sprinkle each with a little chopped parsley.

TO FREEZE Cool quickly after adding the cream and paprika in step 4. Put in freezerproof containers, seal and freeze for up to one month.
TO USE Thaw the chowder overnight in the fridge. Put in a pan, cover and bring to the boil, then simmer on a low heat for 15–20 minutes or until bubbling.

Mediterranean fish soup

PREPARATION TIME: 25 minutes
COOKING TIME: 55 minutes
PER SERVING: 290cals, 9g fat, 14g carbohydrate

SERVES 6

FOR THE FISH STOCK

50ml (2fl oz) olive oil

125g (4oz) each onion, carrot and fennel, roughly
  chopped

450g (1lb) plum tomatoes or 397g can plum tomatoes,
  roughly chopped

Bones from the mixed fish

1 dressed crab, meat removed and shells put to one side

225g (8oz) tiger prawns, peeled, deveined and shells put
  to one side

Few parsley and thyme stalks

Black peppercorns

150ml (¼ pint) dry white wine

FOR THE SOUP

225g (8oz) each onion, fennel and potatoes, finely
  chopped

2 level tsp each fennel seeds and chopped fresh thyme

Pinch of saffron

3 garlic cloves

150ml (¼ pint) vermouth, eg Noilly Prat

3 level tbsp tomato paste

700g (1½lb) mixed fish pieces, eg red mullet, whiting,
  monkfish and John Dory, skinned and filleted and cut
  into 2.5cm (1in) cubes or slices

700g (1½lb) fresh mussels or clams, washed, debearded,
  tapped and any open or damaged ones discarded

Rouille (see opposite) or shop-bought rouille or garlic
  mayonnaise, toasts and grated Gruyère cheese to serve

Try to buy fish and seafood on the day you want to eat it as it spoils very quickly, especially if the weather's hot. When you buy fish it must be absolutely fresh and smell of the sea. The eyes must be bright and clear, the gills bright pink or red and the flesh firm. When you press it with your finger it should not leave an indentation and when you pick it up it should not flop. The fishmonger will scale, clean, fillet or skin fish if you ask him. The ingredients list may look long but this easy fish soup is much quicker to make than most.

1 For the fish stock, heat 25ml (1fl oz) of the olive oil in a large wide pan then add the vegetables, fish bones, fish shells, parsley and thyme stalks and peppercorns. Cook for 4–5 minutes. Add the white wine and boil to reduce by half. Add enough cold water to just cover the shells and vegetables, about 1.1 litres (2 pints). Bring to the boil and simmer for 10–15 minutes, then season with salt and freshly ground black pepper. Strain through a fine sieve into a jug, and put to one side.

2 To make the soup, heat the remaining oil in the stock pan, add the onions, fennel, potatoes, fennel seeds, thyme, saffron and garlic. Cook for 5 minutes, stirring.

3 Add the vermouth and tomato paste and bubble until reduced to a syrupy consistency. Add the fish stock and simmer, uncovered, for 20–25 minutes, skimming off any scum that comes to the surface.

4 Season well and bring to a rolling boil. Add the crabmeat, prawns, mixed fish and mussels or clams to the fish stock. Bring up to the boil and gently simmer for 1–2 minutes, or until the mussels or clams have opened. Discard any that don't open.

5 Serve immediately, with the rouille spread on the toasts and with the grated cheese.

TO PREPARE AHEAD Complete the recipe to the end of step 3, cool quickly, then cover and chill the soup and prepared fish separately.
TO USE Complete the recipe as in step 4.

Rouille

PREPARATION TIME: 5 minutes
PER SERVING: 350cals, 38g fat, 2g carbohydrate

SERVES 6

300ml (½ pint) bought mayonnaise

6 garlic cloves, crushed

4 level tbsp sun-dried tomato paste

2 level tsp harissa or a few drops Tabasco sauce

The traditional accompaniment to fish soups such as the one opposite, or bouillabaisse on page 24, rouille can be made up to 1 week ahead of when you need it; keep it chilled. Harissa is a hot sauce, usually made from chillies, garlic, spices and oil. It's widely available.

1 Mix all the ingredients together in a bowl, cover tightly and chill in the fridge until needed.

Miso mushroom and spinach soup

PREPARATION TIME: 5 minutes
COOKING TIME: 25 minutes
PER SERVING: 60cals, 3g fat, 6g carbohydrate

SERVES 6

1 tbsp vegetable oil

1 medium onion, halved and finely sliced

120g packet shiitake mushrooms, finely sliced

225g bag baby spinach leaves, washed and ready to use

4 x 284ml cartons fresh fish stock

4 tbsp mugi miso (fermented soya beans)

This quick, simple soup has an authentic Japanese flavour.

1 Heat the oil in a large pan and gently sauté the onion for 15 minutes.
2 Add the shiitake mushrooms and cook for 5 minutes, then stir in the spinach and the fish stock. Heat for 3 minutes, then stir in the mugi miso – don't boil the soup as miso is a live culture.
3 Spoon into six bowls and serve.

Bouillabaisse

PREPARATION TIME: 15 minutes
COOKING TIME: 45 minutes
PER SERVING: 200cals, 8g fat, 6g carbohydrate

SERVES 4

3tbsp olive oil
1 onion, sliced
1 leek, sliced
2 sticks celery, sliced
2 garlic cloves, crushed
397g can chopped tomatoes
1 strip of pared orange rind
1 level tbsp sundried tomato paste
½ level tsp fennel seeds
1.1 litres (2 pints) fish stock
Pinch of saffron, soaked in 150ml (¼ pint) boiling water
900g (2lb) mixed fish fillets cut into small pieces,
    eg whiting, John Dory and red mullet, and shellfish,
    eg cooked, peeled prawns and mussels
3 level tbsp chopped fresh mixed parsley and thyme

This classic fish soup originates from Marseilles. The original version uses a lot of olive oil, but in this recipe the calories are reduced by cutting down the amount of oil. If you use mainly white varieties of fish, rather than the oily type, it will also help to keep the calorie count lower. If you like, serve with some rouille (see page 23).

1 Heat the oil in a large pan, then add the onion, leek, celery and garlic and cook for about 5 minutes or until beginning to soften. Add the tomatoes, orange rind, tomato paste and fennel seeds and cook for 1–2 minutes.

2 Add the fish stock with the saffron and its liquid, then season to taste with salt and freshly ground black pepper. Bring to the boil and simmer for about 30 minutes, then adjust the seasoning if necessary.

3 Add the fish and mussels, but not the prawns, and cook for about 5–6 minutes until the fish is just cooked and the mussels have opened – discard any mussels that don't open. Stir in the herbs and prawns, then serve with French bread.

2

CHICKEN & DUCK

EASY RED THAI CHICKEN CURRY

MOROCCAN CHICKEN

CARIBBEAN CHICKEN

MEDITERRANEAN ROAST CHICKEN

CHICKEN WITH CHICKPEAS

SPANISH CHICKEN PARCELS

GLAZED DUCK WITH ROSEMARY AND GARLIC

Easy red Thai chicken curry

PREPARATION TIME: 5 minutes

COOKING TIME: 20 minutes

PER SERVING: 410cals, 28g fat, 5g carbohydrate

SERVES 4

1 tbsp vegetable oil

3 level tbsp red Thai curry paste

4 chicken breasts – around 600g (1lb 5oz) – sliced

400ml can coconut milk

300ml (½ pint) hot chicken or vegetable stock

Juice of 1 lime

200g pack of mixed baby corn and mangetout

2 level tbsp chopped fresh coriander

The red Thai curry paste uses fiery dried bird's eye chillies. Plain rice noodles are a good accompaniment to the dish.

1 Heat the oil in a wok or large pan. Add the curry paste and cook for 2 minutes.

2 Add the chicken breasts and fry gently until browned.

3 Add the coconut milk, stock, lime juice and baby corn to the pan and bring to the boil. Add the mangetout, reduce the heat and simmer for 4–5 minutes until the chicken is cooked. Add the chopped coriander and serve immediately.

Moroccan chicken

PREPARATION TIME: 10 minutes

COOKING TIME: 50 minutes

PER SERVING: 350cals, 15g fat, 18g carbohydrate

SERVES 6

12 chicken pieces, to include thighs, drumsticks and breasts

1 large onion, sliced

2 garlic cloves, crushed

2 level tbsp rose harissa

Large pinch of saffron

1 level tsp salt

1 cinnamon stick

600ml (1 pint) chicken stock

75g (3oz) raisins

2 x 410g cans chickpeas, drained and rinsed

A fragrant and spicy dish, influenced by the tagines of Morocco and Tunisia. This dish uses a variety of harissa with rose. Serve the chicken with warm flatbreads, such as plain naans or pittas. *Illustrated*

1 Heat a large, wide non-stick pan. Add the chicken pieces, skin-side down, and fry until well browned all over. Add the onion and garlic and stir together for 5 minutes.

2 Add the harissa, saffron, salt and the cinnamon stick and season well with freshly ground black pepper. Pour the stock over and bring to the boil, then reduce the heat, cover and simmer gently for 25–30 minutes.

3 Add the raisins and chickpeas and bring to the boil. Simmer uncovered for 5–10 minutes, then serve.

Caribbean chicken

PREPARATION TIME: 40 minutes, plus at least
4 hours marinating
COOKING TIME: 45–50 minutes
PER SERVING: 660cals, 19g fat, 85g carbohydrate

SERVES 5

1.4kg (3lb) medium chicken, without giblets, rinsed and
 dried thoroughly with kitchen paper, or 10 chicken
 pieces – such as thighs, drumsticks, wings or breasts
1 level tbsp ground coriander
2 level tsp ground cumin
1 level tbsp paprika
Pinch of ground nutmeg
1 scotch bonnet bell chilli pepper, deseeded and chopped
1 onion, chopped
5 fresh thyme sprigs, leaves removed
4 garlic cloves, crushed
2tbsp dark soy sauce
Juice of 1 lemon
2tbsp vegetable oil
2 level tbsp light muscovado sugar
350g (12oz) – or pour into a measuring jug up to 450ml
 (¾ pint) – American easy-cook rice
3tbsp dark rum (optional)
25g (1oz) butter
2 x 300g cans black-eyed beans, drained
Few fresh thyme sprigs to garnish

The West Indies is a huge melting pot of cultures, and cooking inspiration is taken from the culinary traditions of India, Africa, France, Spain, China and Holland. This dish, known as a 'pelau' – the Caribbean spelling – uses American easy-cook rice, unlike the aromatic Indian rice dish pullao, which is traditionally cooked with basmati rice. Turkish pilav or pilaff uses long-grain rice, originally brought from China, while traditional Spanish rice dishes are based on short-grain rice.

1 To make 10 chicken portions, cut along the centre of the chicken breast through to the bone. Cut off the breast pieces from each side and divide in two. Turn the chicken over and cut away either side of the backbone and discard. Cut off the wings, remove tips from the legs and discard. Hold each drumstick, twist backwards and cut away from the thigh.

2 Remove the skin from the chicken pieces and discard. Pierce the meat with a knife, put in a container and sprinkle with ½tsp of salt, some freshly ground black pepper, the coriander, cumin, paprika and nutmeg. Add the chilli pepper, onion, thyme and garlic, then pour the soy sauce and lemon juice over and stir to combine. Cover and chill for at least 4 hours.

3 Heat a 3.4 litre (6 pint) heavy-based pan over a medium heat for 2 minutes. Add the vegetable oil and muscovado sugar, then cook over a medium heat for 3 minutes or until it turns a rich golden caramel colour. (Be careful not to overcook it as the mixture will blacken and taste burnt – so watch it very carefully.)

4 Remove the chicken pieces from the marinade and add to the dark golden sugar and oil mixture in the hot pan. Cover and cook over a medium heat for 5 minutes, then turn the chicken and cook, covered, for another 5 minutes until evenly browned. Add the onion and any remaining juices from the marinade. Turn again, then cover and cook for 10 minutes.

5 Add the rice, stir to combine with the chicken, then pour in 900ml (1½ pints) of cold water. Add the rum, if using, the butter and ½tsp salt. Cover with a lid and simmer over a gentle heat, without lifting the lid, for 20 minutes or until the rice is tender and most of the liquid has been absorbed.

6 Add the black-eyed beans to the pan and mix well. Cover and cook for 3–5 minutes until the beans are just warmed through and all the liquid has been absorbed, taking care the rice doesn't stick to the base of the pan. Garnish with the thyme sprigs and serve.

Mediterranean roast chicken

PREPARATION TIME: 35 minutes

COOKING TIME: 1 hour 25 minutes

PER SERVING WITHOUT SKIN: 580cals, 32g fat, 39g carbohydrate

PER SERVING WITH SKIN: 670cals, 43g fat, 39g carbohydrate

SERVES 4

1.2kg (2lb 11½ oz) whole free-range chicken

Juice of 1 lemon, unwaxed, halves reserved

4 level tbsp roughly chopped thyme, stalks reserved, plus extra sprigs

4 level tbsp roughly chopped sage leaves, stalks reserved, plus extra leaves

125g (4oz) butter, softened

900g (2lb) floury potatoes, such as Maris Piper, peeled and cut into even chunks

2tbsp olive oil

2 fennel bulbs, cut into wedges

1 red onion, peeled and cut into wedges

This is a tasty twist on the classic roast. The herby butter placed underneath the skin of the chicken keeps it beautifully moist during cooking.

1 Preheat the oven to 190°C (170°C fan oven) mark 5.

2 Put the chicken on a board and push the lemon halves and herb stalks into the cavity. Ease your fingers under the skin of the neck end to separate the breast skin from the flesh, then push the herbs and most of the butter up under the skin, keeping a little butter to one side. Season well with salt and freshly ground black pepper.

3 Put the potatoes into a roasting tin, drizzle over the olive oil and roast for 5 minutes.

4 Add the chicken to the roasting tin, pour the lemon juice over, then top with extra sage and thyme and the remaining butter.

5 Arrange the fennel and red onion around the chicken. Cook for 1 hour 20 minutes or 20 minutes per 450g (1lb), basting every 20 minutes, until the juices run clear. Carve the chicken and serve with the vegetables.

Chicken with chickpeas

PREPARATION TIME: 10 minutes
COOKING TIME: 45 minutes
PER SERVING: 330cals, 15g fat, 14g carbohydrate

SERVES 4

2tbsp sunflower oil
1 onion, finely chopped
1 level tsp turmeric
4 large skinless chicken breasts
Juice of 1 lemon, or to taste
3 large garlic cloves, crushed
400g can chickpeas, drained and rinsed
Pinch of cayenne pepper
Chopped fresh flat-leafed parsley to garnish

Serve this low-fat dish with some couscous for an easy supper.

1 Heat the oil in a large frying pan, add the onion and fry over a low heat for 5–6 minutes until translucent and softened. Stir in the turmeric.

2 Add the chicken and turn in the turmeric mixture until yellow all over. Add the lemon juice, garlic, 300ml (½ pint) of cold water and season with salt and freshly ground black pepper.

3 Bring to the boil and simmer, covered, for about 20 minutes, then add the chickpeas and continue to simmer for another 5–10 minutes until the chicken is cooked.

4 Remove the chicken with a slotted spoon and keep covered. Bring the remaining liquid and chickpeas to the boil and bubble for 4–5 minutes until the liquid has reduced and thickened. Return the chicken to the pan for 1–2 minutes to heat through, then sprinkle with cayenne pepper. Garnish with the chopped parsley and serve.

Spanish chicken parcels

PREPARATION TIME: 30 minutes
COOKING TIME: 30 minutes
PER SERVING: 330cals, 17g fat, 5g carbohydrate

SERVES 6

12 boneless, skinless thighs – around 900g (2lb)
180g jar pimientos, drained
12 slices chorizo sausage
2tbsp olive oil
1 onion, finely chopped
4 garlic cloves, crushed
230g can chopped tomatoes
4tbsp dry sherry
18 queen green olives

These yummy little chicken pieces are perfect served with some crusty bread.

1 Put the chicken thighs on a board, season well with salt and freshly ground black pepper and put a piece of pimiento inside each one. Wrap a slice of chorizo around the outside and secure with two cocktail sticks. Put to one side.

2 Heat the olive oil in a pan and fry the onion for 10 minutes. Add the garlic and cook for 1 minute. Put the chicken parcels, chorizo-side down, in the pan and brown them all over, cooking for about 10–15 minutes.

3 Add the chopped tomatoes and sherry to the pan and bring to the boil. Simmer for 5 minutes or until the juices run clear. Add the olives, warm through and serve.

Glazed duck with rosemary and garlic

PREPARATION TIME: 20 minutes, plus 1 hour marinating

COOKING TIME: 1 hour

PER SERVING: 660cals, 47g fat, 29g carbohydrate

SERVES 4

4 duck breasts – around 175–200g (6–7oz) each

Finely grated rind and juice of 1 lemon

1 garlic clove, crushed

450g (1lb) new potatoes, scrubbed and halved

125g (4oz) shallots, covered with boiling water for 5 minutes, then peeled and halved if large

225g (8oz) baby leeks, trimmed, or regular leeks cut into 7.5cm (3in) pieces

225g (8oz) small carrots, halved lengthways

2tbsp olive oil

2 level tbsp chopped fresh rosemary

4tsp runny honey

Few fresh rosemary sprigs to garnish

Duck breasts are thick and meaty and here their richness is reduced by the lemon and garlic marinade.

1 Score the skin of the duck breasts with a sharp knife and put them back on the plastic trays they were bought in. Sprinkle over the grated lemon rind and juice, garlic, salt and freshly ground black pepper. Turn several times to coat in the juice mix, cover and leave for 1 hour for the flavours to mingle.

2 Preheat the oven to 220°C (200°C fan oven) mark 7. Put the potatoes, shallots, leeks and carrots into a large roasting tin. Toss together in the olive oil, then sprinkle with sea salt and chopped rosemary. Roast for 30 minutes.

3 Put the duck breasts on a metal rack, smear the skin with the honey and sprinkle generously with sea salt. Remove the tray of vegetables from the oven and turn them, draining off any oil. Position the duck on the rack over the vegetables. Roast for 25–30 minutes, or until the duck is brown and tender and the vegetables tender and a little charred.

4 Put the duck on a serving dish, surround with the vegetables, garnish with the rosemary sprigs and serve.

3

FISH & SEAFOOD

THAI RED CURRY WITH PRAWNS

STIR-FRIED PRAWNS WITH PAK CHOI

PRAWN PROVENÇAL

STIR-FRIED PRAWNS AND NOODLES IN YELLOW BEAN SAUCE

MOULES MARINIÈRE

MUSSELS WITH CIDER AND RED ONIONS

MUSSEL AND POTATO STEW

TERIYAKI SALMON WITH SPINACH AND NOODLES

SEAFOOD GUMBO

SEAFOOD STEW

SEAFOOD CHOWDER

SPICY MONKFISH STEW

MEDITERRANEAN FISH STEW

SMOKED FISH PIE

Thai red curry with prawns

PREPARATION TIME: 15 minutes

COOKING TIME: 25 minutes

PER SERVING: 260cals, 19g fat, 8g carbohydrate

SERVES 4

1 tbsp oil

1 onion, finely sliced

250g pack baby aubergines, halved lengthways

1–2tbsp red Thai curry paste

400ml can coconut milk

200ml (7fl oz) hot fish stock

1 tbsp Thai fish sauce – nam pla (optional)

200g (7oz) raw tiger prawns, peeled

3 level tbsp roughly chopped fresh coriander, plus extra
   to garnish

In Thailand, this might be made with tiny pea aubergines – look out for them in Thai food shops. Regular aubergines cut into sticks make a suitable substitute. Thai fish sauce (nam pla) is a salty, fermented sauce with a distinctive aroma. It's used as a seasoning, condiment and sauce.

1 Heat the oil in a wok or large pan and fry the onion over a medium heat until golden. Add the aubergines and fry for a further 5 minutes until pale brown.

2 Add the curry paste and stir to coat the vegetables, then continue to cook for 1 minute.

3 Add the coconut milk, stock and fish sauce, if using, then bring to the boil and simmer for 5 minutes.

4 Add the prawns and season generously with salt and freshly ground black pepper. Simmer until the prawns have turned pink – just a couple of minutes.

5 Add the coriander and stir, then transfer to large warmed bowls and serve garnished with the extra chopped coriander.

Stir-fried prawns with pak choi

PREPARATION TIME: 30 minutes

COOKING TIME: 6 minutes

PER SERVING: 140cals, 8g fat, 6g carbohydrate

SERVES 4

2tbsp vegetable oil

2 garlic cloves, thinly sliced

1 stem lemongrass, cut in half and bruised

2 kaffir lime leaves, torn into small pieces

1 small red onion, thinly sliced

1 hot red chilli, deseeded and thinly sliced

4cm (1½in) piece fresh root ginger, cut into long thin shreds

1 level tbsp coriander seeds, lightly crushed

450g (1lb) large raw prawns, peeled and deveined (see recipe introduction)

175g (6oz) mangetout, halved diagonally

225g (8oz) pak choi or Chinese mustard cabbage, trimmed, damaged leaves discarded and leaves torn into pieces

2tbsp Thai fish sauce (nam pla)

Juice of 1 lime, or to taste

Fried sliced red chilli, deseeded, to garnish

Pak choi is a member of the cabbage family, but don't let memories of boiled school cabbage put you off – it's full of nutrients and is delicious stir-fried. To devein raw prawns, just run a knife down the middle of the back of each prawn and remove the thin black vein. If using cooked prawns instead of raw, add with the lime juice and heat for 1 minute at step 3.

1 Heat the oil in a wok or large frying pan. Add the garlic, lemongrass, lime leaves, onion, chilli, ginger and coriander seeds, and stir-fry for 2 minutes.

2 Add the prawns, mangetout and pak choi or cabbage and stir-fry until the vegetables are cooked but still crisp and the prawns are pink and opaque, about 2–3 minutes.

3 Add the fish sauce and lime juice, and heat through for 1 minute. Discard the lemongrass. Serve immediately while the vegetables are crisp, garnished with sliced red chilli.

Prawn provençal

PREPARATION TIME: 20 minutes
COOKING TIME: 25 minutes
PER SERVING FOR 4: 320cals, 12g fat,
12g carbohydrate
PER SERVING FOR 6: 210cals, 8g fat,
8g carbohydrate

SERVES 4 AS A MAIN DISH OR 6 AS A STARTER

3tbsp olive oil

4 shallots or 1 small onion, finely chopped

3 garlic cloves, crushed or chopped

1 level tbsp tomato paste

150ml (¼ pint) white wine

700g (1½lb) tomatoes, preferably plum tomatoes, peeled,
    deseeded and roughly chopped

Bouquet garni

700g (1½lb) raw, peeled tiger prawns or peeled
    langoustine tails

Serve this classic dish with crusty bread as a starter or with rice
and salad as a main course.

1 Heat the olive oil in a large frying pan, add the shallots and cook for
1–2 minutes. Add the garlic and cook for 30 seconds before adding the
tomato paste; cook for 1 minute. Pour in the white wine, bring to the
boil and bubble for about 10 minutes until very well reduced and syrupy.

2 Add the tomatoes and bouquet garni, then season to taste with salt and
freshly ground black pepper. Bring to the boil and simmer gently for
5 minutes or until pulpy.

3 Add the prawns or langoustine tails to the hot sauce, then bring back to
the boil and simmer gently, stirring, for 1–2 minutes or until the prawns
are pink and just cooked through to the centre. Serve immediately.

TO PREPARE AHEAD Complete the recipe to the end of step 2, cool
quickly, then cover and chill for up to two days.
TO USE Bring the sauce to the boil, then complete the recipe as in step 3.

Stir-fried prawns and noodles in yellow bean sauce

PREPARATION TIME: 10 minutes
COOKING TIME: 5 minutes, plus 4 minutes standing
PER SERVING: 340cals, 6g fat, 50g carbohydrate

SERVES 4

250g pack medium egg noodles

1tbsp stir-fry oil or sesame oil

1 garlic clove, sliced

1 level tsp freshly grated ginger

1 bunch spring onions, trimmed and each stem cut into
    four lengthways

250g pack frozen raw peeled tiger prawns, thawed

200g (7oz) pak choi, leaves removed and the white base
    cut into thick slices

160g jar Chinese yellow bean stir-fry sauce

You can't get much easier than this – it's ready and on the table in
20 minutes. *Illustrated on page 2.*

1 Put the noodles in a bowl, pour over 2 litres (3½ pints) of boiling water
and leave to soak for 4 minutes. Drain and set aside.

2 Heat the oil in a wok, add the garlic and grated ginger and stir-fry for
30 seconds. Add the spring onions and prawns and cook for 2 minutes.

3 Add the chopped white part of the pak choi and the jar of sauce. Fill the
empty sauce jar with boiling water from the kettle and pour this into the
wok, too.

4 Add the noodles to the pan and continue to cook for 1 minute, tossing
every now and then to heat through. Finally, stir in the green pak choi
leaves and serve.

Moules marinière

PREPARATION TIME: 20 minutes
COOKING TIME: 20 minutes
PER SERVING: 270cals, 15g fat, 9g carbohydrate

SERVES 4

25g (1oz) butter
4 shallots, finely chopped
2 garlic cloves, crushed
200ml (7fl oz) dry white wine
2 level tbsp freshly chopped flat-leafed parsley
2kg (4½lb) fresh mussels, washed, debearded, tapped and any open or damaged ones discarded
100ml (3½fl oz) thick single cream

A bowl of fresh mussels cooked in white wine and cream makes a luxurious one-pot supper dish that's really easy to put together.

1 Heat the butter in a large non-stick lidded frying pan and sauté the shallots over a medium high heat for about 10 minutes or until soft.

2 Add the garlic, wine and half the parsley to the pan and bring to the boil. Tip in the mussels and reduce the heat a little. Cover and cook for about 5 minutes or until all the shells have opened; discard any mussels that don't open.

3 Lift the mussels out with a slotted spoon into serving bowls and cover with foil to keep warm. Add the cream to the stock, season with salt and freshly ground black pepper and cook for 1–2 minutes to heat through.

4 Pour a little sauce over the mussels and sprinkle with the rest of the parsley.

Mussels with cider and red onions

PREPARATION TIME: 20 minutes
COOKING TIME: 30 minutes
PER SERVING: 650cals, 53g fat, 13g carbohydrate

SERVES 4

75g (3oz) butter
450g (1lb) red onions, finely chopped
3 garlic cloves
300ml (½ pint) cider
2kg (4½lb) fresh mussels, washed, debearded, tapped and any open or damaged ones discarded
284ml carton double cream
Fresh parsley sprigs to garnish (optional)

Use the freshest possible mussels for this quick supper dish. It also makes a delicious starter.

1 Melt the butter in a large heavy-based pan. Add the red onions and cook, stirring, for 10 minutes or until soft, then add the garlic and cook for a further 2 minutes. Stir in the cider. Bring to the boil, then add the mussels. Cover and cook for 4–5 minutes or until the mussels have opened.

2 Remove the mussels with a large draining spoon and put them into their serving bowls, discarding any mussels that haven't opened. Bring the liquor to the boil with the cream then bubble for 10 minutes or until reduced and lightly syrupy.

3 Pour the sauce over the mussels and season to taste with salt and freshly ground black pepper. Serve immediately, garnished with some fresh parsley if you like.

Mussel and potato stew

PREPARATION TIME: 15 minutes
COOKING TIME: 20 minutes
PER SERVING: 590cals, 35g fat, 45g carbohydrate

SERVES 4

25g (1oz) butter
200g pack rindless back bacon rashers, cut into strips
700g (1½lb) white potatoes, cut into large chunks
198g can sweetcorn kernels, drained
1kg (2¼lb) fresh mussels, washed, debearded, tapped
   and any open or damaged ones discarded
142ml carton single cream
1 level tbsp chopped fresh parsley

Most of us think of mussels as a real culinary treat, but in fact they're relatively cheap – and speedy to cook, too. Ideally, to ensure their freshness, buy them on the same day as you are going to cook them. However, they will keep for a day or two in the fridge.

1 Melt the butter in a large pan, add the bacon and cook, stirring, until the strips separate.

2 Add the potatoes and 150ml (¼ pint) of cold water to the pan and season lightly with salt and freshly ground black pepper. Cover with a tight-fitting lid and cook for 10 minutes or until the potatoes are almost tender.

3 Add the sweetcorn and mussels to the pan, cover, bring to the boil and simmer for 2–3 minutes or until the mussels open. Discard any mussels that don't open. Add the cream and the chopped parsley and serve in warmed bowls.

Teriyaki salmon with spinach and noodles

PREPARATION TIME: 10 minutes, plus 1 hour marinating
COOKING TIME: 10 minutes
PER SERVING: 450cals, 28g fat, 18g carbohydrate

SERVES 4

500g (1¼lb) salmon fillet, cut into 1cm (½in) slices
3tbsp teriyaki sauce
3tbsp light soy sauce
2tbsp vegetable oil
1tbsp sesame oil
1 level tbsp chopped fresh chives
2 level tsp grated fresh root ginger
2 garlic cloves, crushed
350g bag baby spinach leaves
3 x 160g packets of yakisoba noodles
Furikake seasoning

A mixture of sesame seeds and seaweed, furikake makes a pretty garnish and adds a salty toasted flavour. It's sold in the Japanese section of supermarkets.

1 Gently mix the salmon with the teriyaki sauce, then cover, chill and leave to marinate for 1 hour.

2 Mix together the soy sauce, 1tbsp of the vegetable oil, the sesame oil, chives, ginger and garlic. Put to one side.

3 Heat the rest of the vegetable oil in a wok. Lift the salmon from the marinade and add to the pan. Cook over a high heat until lightly coloured. Push to the side of the pan.

4 Add the spinach, cover and cook for 2 minutes over a high heat until wilted. Push to the side of the pan and add the noodles, along with 6tbsp of cold water and the seasoning sachets from the noodle packets. Cook, stirring, until the noodles have loosened and warmed through.

5 Add the soy sauce mixture and stir to combine, mixing in the spinach as you do so but leaving the salmon at the side of the pan.

6 Divide the noodles among four deep bowls, then lay the salmon on top. Sprinkle with furikake seasoning and serve.

Seafood gumbo

PREPARATION TIME: 10 minutes

COOKING TIME: 30 minutes

PER SERVING: 570cals, 34g fat, 33g carbohydrate

SERVES 4

125g (4oz) butter

50g (2oz) plain flour

1–2 level tbsp Cajun spice

1 onion, chopped

1 green pepper, cored, deseeded and chopped

5 spring onions, sliced

1 level tbsp chopped fresh parsley

1 garlic clove, crushed

1 beef tomato, chopped

125g (4oz) garlic sausage, finely sliced

75g (3oz) American easy-cook rice

1.1 litres (2 pints) vegetable stock

450g (1lb) okra, sliced

1 bay leaf

1 thyme sprig

2 level tsp salt

¼ level tsp cayenne pepper

Juice of ½ lemon

4 cloves

500g (1¼lb) frozen mixed seafood – containing mussels, squid and prawns – thawed and drained

Based on a Creole dish, this is halfway between a soup and a stew. Okra, or lady's fingers, is an essential ingredient as it adds a lovely silky texture, and, in fact, the name gumbo is derived from the African word for okra.

1 Heat the butter in a 2.5 litre (4¼–4½ pint) heavy-based pan. Add the flour and Cajun spice and cook for 1–2 minutes or until golden brown. Add the onion, green pepper, spring onions, parsley and garlic. Cook for 5 minutes.

2 Add the tomato, garlic sausage and easy-cook rice to the pan and stir well to coat. Add the stock, okra, bay leaf, thyme, the salt, cayenne pepper, lemon juice and cloves and season with freshly ground black pepper. Bring to the boil and simmer, covered, for 12 minutes or until the rice is tender.

3 Add the seafood and cook for 2 minutes to heat through. Serve the gumbo in deep bowls.

Seafood stew

PREPARATION TIME: 15 minutes
COOKING TIME: 35 minutes
PER SERVING: 340cals, 6g fat, 40g carbohydrate

SERVES 4

1 tbsp olive oil

1 onion, finely sliced

450g (1lb) Desirée potatoes, peeled and chopped into
    2cm (¾in) pieces

1–2 level tbsp sundried tomato paste

400g can chopped plum tomatoes in rich juice

300ml (½ pint) hot fish or vegetable stock

2 sprigs fresh rosemary, plus extra to garnish

1 red pepper, diced

1 courgette, diced

400g bag frozen seafood, thawed and drained

4tbsp pesto and French bread to serve

This dish is full of flavour, and fresh, crunchy French bread is the perfect accompaniment to soak up all the juices. *Illustrated*

1 Heat the oil and fry the onion over a medium heat for 5 minutes until golden. Add the potatoes and sundried tomato paste and stir-fry for 1–2 minutes.

2 Pour the plum tomatoes and hot stock into the pan, stir together and season well with salt and freshly ground black pepper. Add the rosemary, then cover and bring to the boil. Simmer for 15 minutes.

3 Add the diced pepper and courgette to the pan and cook for 5 minutes.

4 Add the seafood, stir and continue to cook for 5 minutes. Spoon the pesto into individual pots or one bowl.

5 Spoon the seafood stew into the serving pots or bowl, garnish each one with a sprig of fresh rosemary and serve immediately with the pesto and French bread.

Seafood chowder

PREPARATION TIME: 10 minutes
COOKING TIME: 15 minutes
PER SERVING: 380cals, 20g fat, 46g carbohydrate

SERVES 4

25g (1oz) butter

1 bunch spring onions, chopped

2 level tbsp mustard powder

2tbsp tomato paste

415g can butter beans, drained and rinsed

568ml carton milk

50g (2oz) instant mashed potato

50g (2oz) Cheddar cheese, grated

300g (11oz) packet mixed cooked seafood

Traditional American chowders are very, very thick – the instant mashed potato is a speedy way of thickening the milk.

1 Heat the butter in a pan and fry the onions with the mustard powder for 2 minutes.

2 Add the tomato paste and beans and fry for 1 minute. Add the milk and bring to the boil.

3 Lower the heat, sprinkle in the potato and stir until blended. Add the cheese and seafood. Simmer for 2–3 minutes, stirring – do not boil. Pour into bowls and serve.

Spicy monkfish stew

PREPARATION TIME: 10 minutes

COOKING TIME: 35 minutes

PER SERVING: 160cals, 3g fat, 18g carbohydrate

SERVES 6

1 tbsp olive oil

1 onion, finely sliced

1 tbsp tom yum soup paste

450g (1lb) potatoes, cut into 2cm (¾in) chunks

400g can chopped tomatoes in rich tomato juice

600ml (1 pint) hot fish stock

450g (1lb) monkfish, cut into 2cm (¾in) chunks

200g bag washed ready-to-eat baby spinach

Monkfish is a low-in-fat, firm-textured fish with a wonderful sweet flavour – pricey, but worth it.

1 Heat the oil in a pan and fry the onion over a medium heat for 5 minutes, until golden.

2 Add the Tom Yum paste and potatoes and stir-fry for 1 minute. Add the tomatoes and hot stock, season well with salt and freshly ground black pepper and cover. Bring to the boil then simmer, partially covered, for 15 minutes or until the potatoes are just tender.

3 Add the monkfish to the pan and continue to simmer for 5–10 minutes or until the fish is cooked. Add the baby spinach leaves and stir through until wilted.

4 Spoon the fish stew into warmed bowls and serve immediately with crusty bread.

Mediterranean fish stew

PREPARATION TIME: 30 minutes
COOKING TIME: 40 minutes
PER SERVING: 430cals, 21g fat, 23g carbohydrate

MAKES 2 MEALS FOR 4

4tbsp olive oil

1 large Spanish onion, finely chopped

3 garlic cloves, chopped

1 level tbsp tomato paste

Large pinch of saffron

2 large potatoes – about 500g (1lb 2oz) – peeled and cut
    into large chunks

1.4 litres (2½ pints) well-flavoured fish stock

1 head fennel, thinly sliced

6 tomatoes, deseeded and sliced

3 level tbsp plain flour

½ level tsp cayenne pepper

450g (1lb) cod fillet, skinned and cut into 4cm (1½in)
    chunks

225g (8oz) monkfish tail, trimmed and cut into 4cm
    (1½in) chunks

225g (8oz) raw tiger prawns, deveined

2tbsp brandy, optional

3 level tbsp roughly chopped flat-leafed parsley

1 bag ciabatta croûtes

1 jar rouille paste (or see page 23), or 1 jar garlic
    mayonnaise

50g (2oz) freshly grated Parmesan cheese

A heavenly combination of cod, monkfish and tiger prawns, served in a saffron broth – lovely as a light lunch, with crisp croûtons and a delicious garlic mayonnaise. Ideally, choose fresh fish, but don't worry if you can find only pre-frozen varieties – it's all cooked in this recipe so it will be safe to refreeze.

1 Heat the oil in a large pan, add the onion and cook over a very low heat for 10 minutes or until soft. Add the garlic, tomato paste and saffron and cook for 2 minutes.

2 Add the potatoes and fish stock, bring to the boil, reduce the heat and simmer for 15–20 minutes or until the potatoes are nearly cooked. Add the fennel and tomatoes and cook for a further 5 minutes.

3 Put the flour and cayenne pepper into a large plastic bag and season with salt and freshly ground black pepper. Add the cod and monkfish and toss together until completely coated. Tip into a sieve and shake away any excess flour.

4 Add the fish to the simmering stew and poach gently for 3 minutes until cooked. Don't allow it to boil too fiercely as the fish will break up. Add the prawns and cook for 1 minute or until pink.

5 Pour the brandy into a ladle, hold over a gas flame, ignite with a match and, when subdued, pour into the stew. Season to taste with salt and freshly ground black pepper, then add the chopped parsley to the pan. Serve with the croûtes spread with rouille or mayonnaise and topped with Parmesan.

TO FREEZE Complete the recipe to the end of step 4, then add the brandy. Cool the stew quickly, pack in a freezerproof container, seal and freeze for up to three months.
TO USE Thaw overnight at cool room temperature. Put in a pan and reheat gently, add the chopped parsley and serve as above.

Smoked fish pie

PREPARATION TIME: 10 minutes
COOKING TIME: 30 minutes
PER SERVING: 640cals, 43g fat, 39g carbohydrate

SERVES 4

200ml tub crème fraîche

450g (1lb) smoked haddock, skinned (ask your fishmonger to do this) and cut into small chunks

15g (½oz) plain flour

20g packet fresh flat-leafed parsley, roughly chopped

375g pack ready-rolled puff pastry

Smoked fish has such a powerful flavour that little else is needed in this wonderful puff pastry pie. Toss with lots of crème fraîche and flat-leafed parsley for a no-effort filling and you'll have a great midweek supper for friends.

1 Put a large shallow baking sheet in the oven and preheat to 230°C (210°C fan oven) mark 8.

2 Put 1tsp crème fraîche to one side. Put the rest in a bowl with the haddock, flour and parsley and mix together. Season with plenty of freshly ground black pepper and a little salt.

3 Unroll the pastry on to a second baking tray. Brush the edges of the pastry with water. Spoon the fish mixture evenly over half of the pastry, leaving a border along the wet edges. Fold the pastry to make an envelope, press the edges together and crimp to seal.

4 Mix the reserved crème fraîche with 1tsp cold water and brush over the pastry to glaze. Slash the pastry diagonally with a sharp knife to allow any steam to escape.

5 Put the baking tray on top of the hot one in the oven and cook for 30 minutes or until piping hot and golden brown.

4

BEEF, PORK & LAMB

BEEF BRAISED WITH SWEET ONIONS AND GUINNESS

PEPPERED WINTER STEW

BEEF JAMBALAYA

BEEF CASSEROLE WITH BLACK OLIVES

EASY CHILLI CON CARNE

CREAMY PARMA HAM AND ARTICHOKE TAGLIATELLE

SPICY SAUSAGE AND PASTA SUPPER

SAUSAGES WITH ROASTED POTATO AND ONION WEDGES

SPICY BEAN AND SAUSAGE CASSEROLE

CHORIZO SAUSAGE AND POTATO PAN-FRY

CHORIZO SAUSAGE AND CHICKPEA STEW

PAN-FRIED PORK CHOPS WITH LENTILS

PORK CHOPS WITH MUSTARD SAUCE

HONEY PORK WITH ROAST POTATOES AND APPLES

ROASTED PARSNIPS WITH LEEKS, APPLE AND BACON

PORK TENDERLOIN WITH CREAMY MUSTARD SAUCE

BRAISED LAMB SHANKS WITH CANNELLINI BEANS

LUXURY LAMB AND LEEK HOT POT

LAMB WITH SPICED AUBERGINE AND SPINACH

ONE-POT ROAST LAMB WITH SMOKY BACON PASTA

Beef braised with sweet onions and Guinness

PREPARATION TIME: 10 minutes
COOKING TIME: 2½ hours
PER SERVING: 600cals, 36g fat, 16g carbohydrate

SERVES 4

3tbsp olive oil

4 braising steaks – about 700g (1½lb) total weight

175g (6oz) rashers of streaky bacon, sliced

225g (8oz) button onions or shallots, halved

225g (8oz) brown-cap or field mushrooms, sliced

2 garlic cloves, crushed

2 level tbsp plain flour

15g packet dried mushrooms, eg porcini, rinsed and
    soaked in warm water

440ml can Guinness

2tbsp Worcestershire sauce

2 level tsp dried thyme

Large pinch of sugar

Choose steaks that have a fine marbling of fat throughout. This is necessary to help tenderise the meat during cooking. The Guinness adds a creamy flavour to the dish; the alcohol is cooked off in the braising.

1 Preheat the oven to 170°C (150°C fan oven) mark 3. Heat 1tbsp of the olive oil in a 3.4 litre (6 pint) shallow flameproof casserole and fry the steaks on a high heat to seal and brown on both sides. Set aside. Add the bacon and fry until beginning to brown. Set aside.

2 Heat the remaining oil and fry the onions or shallots for about 2–3 minutes or until beginning to brown. Add the fresh mushrooms and cook stirring, for 1–2 minutes then add the garlic and fry for a further 1 minute.

3 Add the flour and stir well to coat the mushrooms and onion. Add the soaked mushrooms and their soaking liquor, the Guinness, Worcestershire sauce, thyme and sugar. Bring to the boil, then reduce the heat to a gentle simmer.

4 Add the steaks and bacon and push down into the liquid. Cover with a tightly fitting lid.

5 Put the casserole in the oven and cook for about 2 hours or until the steaks are tender.

Peppered winter stew

PREPARATION TIME: 20 minutes
COOKING TIME: 2 hours 25 minutes
PER SERVING: 480cals, 18g fat, 25g carbohydrate

SERVES 6

25g (1oz) plain flour

900g (2lb) stewing venison, beef or lamb, cut into 4cm
 (1½in) cubes

5tbsp oil

225g (8oz) button onions or shallots, peeled with root
 end intact

225g (8oz) onion, finely chopped

4 garlic cloves, crushed

2 level tbsp tomato paste

125ml (4fl oz) red wine vinegar

75cl bottle red wine

2 level tbsp redcurrant jelly

1 small bunch thyme

4 bay leaves

1 level tbsp coarsely ground black pepper

6 cloves

600–900ml (1–1½ pints) beef stock

900g (2lb) mixed root vegetables, such as carrots,
 parsnips, turnips and celeriac, cut into 4cm (1½in)
 chunks, carrots cut a little smaller

Few fresh thyme sprigs to garnish

This peppery winter casserole makes a warming meal on a cold day. Remember, button onions are much easier to peel if soaked in boiling water for a minute or two.

1 Put the flour into a plastic bag, season with salt and freshly ground black pepper then toss the meat in it.

2 Heat 3tbsp of the oil in a large deep flameproof casserole and brown the meat well in small batches. Remove and put to one side.

3 Heat the remaining oil and fry the button onions or shallots for 5 minutes or until golden. Add the chopped onion and the garlic and cook, stirring, until soft and golden. Add the tomato paste and cook for a further 2 minutes, then add the vinegar and wine and bring to the boil. Bubble for 10 minutes.

4 Add the redcurrant jelly, thyme, bay leaves, pepper, cloves and meat to the pan and enough stock to barely cover the meat. Bring to the boil, cover and cook at 180°C (160°C fan oven) mark 4 for 1¾–2¼ hours or until the meat is very tender.

5 Serve the stew from the casserole, garnished with the thyme sprigs.

TO FREEZE Complete the recipe to the end of step 4. Cool quickly and put in a freezerproof container. Seal and freeze for up to one month.
TO USE Thaw overnight at cool room temperature. Add an extra 150ml (¼ pint) stock. Bring to the boil. Cover and reheat stew at 180°C (160°C fan oven) mark 4 for 30 minutes.

Beef jambalaya

PREPARATION TIME: 10 minutes
COOKING TIME: 40 minutes
PER SERVING: 600cals, 25g fat, 63g carbohydrate

SERVES 4

275g (10oz) fillet steak, cut into thin strips

4 level tsp mild chilli powder

4tbsp oil

140g (4½oz) pack chorizo sausage, sliced and cut into
    strips, or 125g (4oz) cubed

2 sticks celery, cut into 5cm (2in) strips

2 red peppers, cut into 5cm (2in) strips

150g (5oz) onions, roughly chopped

2 garlic cloves, crushed

275g (10oz) long-grain white rice

1 level tbsp tomato paste

1 level tbsp ground ginger

2 level tsp Cajun seasoning

900ml (1½ pints) beef stock

8 large cooked prawns, shelled

Salad leaves such as lamb's lettuce to serve

Jambalaya is a traditional Creole dish, similar to paella but with more spice. It's great with a crisp, green salad and a sharp lemon dressing. If you like your food really hot and spicy, add Tabasco sauce to taste at the end of step 4. Alternatively, allow your guests to add their own. If you find the dish too spicy, serve it with a little soured cream as this will take away some of the heat. Once the rice has come to the boil, the pan can be transferred to the oven and cooked at 170°C (150°C fan oven) mark 3 for 20 minutes, but remember to stir it occasionally.

1 Put the sliced steak into a plastic bag with 1 level tsp each mild chilli powder and freshly ground black pepper, seal and shake to mix.

2 Heat 1tbsp of the oil in a large frying pan and cook the chorizo until golden. Add the celery and peppers to the pan and cook for 3–4 minutes or until just beginning to soften and brown. Remove from the pan and set aside. Add 2tbsp of the oil to the pan and fry the steak in batches; set aside and keep warm.

3 Add a little more oil to the pan if necessary and cook the onions until transparent. Add the garlic, rice, tomato paste, remaining chilli powder, the ground ginger and Cajun seasoning, then cook for 2 minutes until the rice turns translucent. Stir in the stock, season with salt and bring to the boil. Cover and simmer for about 20 minutes (see above), stirring occasionally, until the rice is tender and most of the liquid has been absorbed (add a little more water during cooking if necessary).

4 Add the reserved steak, chorizo, peppers, celery and the prawns. Heat gently, stirring, until piping hot. Adjust the seasoning and serve with the salad leaves.

Beef casserole with black olives

PREPARATION TIME: 40 minutes
COOKING TIME: 2 hours 10 minutes
PER SERVING: 690cals, 43g fat, 8g carbohydrate

SERVES 6

6tbsp oil

1.1kg (2½lb) stewing steak, preferably in one piece, cut
    into 4cm (1½in) cubes

350g (12oz) streaky bacon rashers, preferably unsmoked,
    rind removed and sliced into thin strips

450g (1lb) onions, roughly chopped

3 large garlic cloves

2 level tbsp tomato paste

110ml (4fl oz) brandy

1 level tbsp plain flour

150ml (¼ pint) red wine

300ml (½ pint) beef stock

Bouquet garni

225g (8oz) flat mushrooms, quartered if large and
    covered

125g (4oz) black olives

Sprigs of fresh flat-leafed parsley to garnish

This is a hearty casserole that improves if it's eaten the day after it's cooked. Instead of streaky bacon rashers – and to save time – use pre-cut bacon lardons. Serve with some garlic bread.

1 Heat half the oil in a large flameproof casserole. On a high heat, brown the stewing steak in batches until it's a dark chestnut brown; remove and keep warm. Add the bacon lardons to the casserole and fry until they are golden brown, then add them to the beef. Add the remaining oil and cook the onions over a moderate heat for 10–15 minutes or until they are golden brown. Add the garlic, fry for 30 seconds, then mix in the tomato paste. Cook, stirring, for 1–2 minutes, then pour in the brandy.

2 Preheat the oven to 170°C (150°C fan oven) mark 3. Bring the casserole to the boil and bubble to reduce by half, then add the plain flour and mix until smooth. Pour in the red wine, bring back to the boil and bubble for 1 minute. Return the stewing steak and bacon to the casserole, then add enough stock to barely cover the meat. Add the bouquet garni. Bring to the boil, then cover, put in the oven and cook for 1¼–1½ hours or until the stewing steak is tender. Add the mushrooms and cook for a further 4–5 minutes.

3 Just before serving, remove the bouquet garni from the casserole and stir in the black olives. Serve immediately, garnished with the parsley sprigs.

TO PREPARE AHEAD Complete the recipe to the end of step 2, cool quickly, then cover and chill for up to two days.
TO USE Bring the casserole slowly to the boil and cook at 180°C (160°C fan oven) mark 4 for 15–20 minutes or until heated through. Complete the recipe.
TO FREEZE Complete the recipe to the end of step 2. Cool quickly and put in a freezerproof container. Seal and freeze for up to one month.
TO USE Thaw the beef casserole overnight at cool room temperature. Put in a pan and bring slowly to the boil and reheat at 180°C (160°C fan oven) mark 4 for 20–25 minutes. Complete the recipe.

Easy chilli con carne

PREPARATION TIME: 15 minutes
COOKING TIME: 45 minutes
PER SERVING: 650cals, 34g fat, 45g carbohydrate

SERVES 4

1 tbsp oil
1 onion, chopped
1 garlic clove, crushed
450g (1lb) lean minced beef
425g can kidney beans, drained and rinsed
440g jar tomato pasta sauce
2 tbsp Worcestershire sauce
1 tbsp chilli sauce
4 tomatoes, chopped
½ iceberg lettuce, shredded
125g (4oz) Cheddar cheese, grated
125g (4oz) tortilla chips
Soured cream to serve

Tortillas are everyday food in Mexico; tortilla chips are the fried version of the soft tortilla bread.

1 Heat the oil in a pan and fry the onion until soft.
2 Add the garlic and minced beef to the pan and fry over a high heat for 5 minutes to brown. Stir in the kidney beans, pasta sauce, Worcestershire and chilli sauce and bring to the boil. Simmer, covered, for 30 minutes.
3 Serve with tomatoes, lettuce, cheese, tortilla chips and topped with spoonfuls of soured cream.

Creamy Parma ham and artichoke tagliatelle

PREPARATION TIME: 5 minutes
COOKING TIME: 10–15 minutes
PER SERVING: 1000cals, 58g fat, 97g carbohydrate

SERVES 4

500g pack dried tagliatelle
500ml tub crème fraîche
280g jar roasted artichoke hearts, drained and halved
80g pack Parma ham (6 slices), torn into strips
2 level tbsp freshly chopped sage leaves, plus extra leaves to garnish
40g (1½oz) Parmesan (use a vegetable peeler to make shavings)

The easiest way to create a luscious and instant creamy sauce is to add a tub of crème fraîche to pasta, then stir in some special ready-to-use ingredients for a luxurious combination that even non-cooks can achieve. *Illustrated*

1 Bring a large pan of water to the boil. Add the pasta, cover and bring back to the boil, then remove the lid, turn the heat down to low and simmer according to the instructions on the pack.
2 Drain the pasta well, leaving a ladleful of the cooking water in the pan, then put the pasta back in the pan.
3 Add the crème fraîche, artichoke hearts, Parma ham and chopped sage and stir everything together. Season well with salt and freshly ground black pepper.
4 Spoon the pasta into warmed bowls, sprinkle the Parmesan shavings over each portion and garnish with sage leaves. Serve immediately.

Spicy sausage and pasta supper

PREPARATION TIME: 20 minutes
COOKING TIME: 30 minutes
PER SERVING FOR 4: 780cals, 45g fat,
47g carbohydrate
PER SERVING FOR 6: 520cals, 30g fat,
31g carbohydrate

SERVES 4–6

1 tbsp olive oil
200g (7oz) salami, sliced
225g (8oz) onion, finely chopped
50g (2oz) celery, finely chopped
2 garlic cloves, crushed
400g can pimientos, drained, rinsed and chopped
400g passata or can chopped tomatoes
125g (4oz) sundried tomatoes drained from oil
600ml (1 pint) hot chicken or vegetable stock
300ml (½ pint) red wine
1 level tbsp sugar
75g (3oz) small dried pasta shapes
400g can borlotti beans, drained and rinsed
284ml carton soured cream
175g (6oz) freshly grated Parmesan cheese
Chopped fresh flat-leafed parsley to garnish

A substantial one-pot meal that all the family will enjoy.

1 Heat the oil in a large pan and fry the sausage for 5 minutes or until golden and crisp. Drain on absorbent kitchen paper.

2 Fry the onion and celery in the hot oil for 10 minutes or until soft and golden. Add the garlic and fry for 1 minute. Return the sausage with the pimientos, passata, sundried tomatoes, stock, red wine and sugar. Bring to the boil.

3 Stir in the pasta, return to the boil, cover and simmer for about 10 minutes or until the pasta is cooked through.

4 Stir in the beans and simmer for 3–4 minutes. Top up with more stock if the pasta is not tender when the liquid has been absorbed. Season with salt and freshly ground black pepper.

5 Ladle into bowls and serve topped with soured cream and plenty of Parmesan cheese, and garnished with the chopped parsley.

TO PREPARE AHEAD Prepare the recipe to the end of step 3 up to one day ahead, cool quickly, cover and chill.
TO USE Return to the boil, stir in the pasta and complete the recipe.

Sausages with roasted potato and onion wedges

PREPARATION TIME: 10 minutes
COOKING TIME: 1 hour 20 minutes
PER SERVING: 490cals, 26g fat, 53g carbohydrate

SERVES 4

900g (2lb) Desirée potatoes, cut into wedges
4tbsp olive oil
3–4 rosemary sprigs (optional)
2 red onions, each cut into eight wedges
8 sausages

This doesn't take long to prepare – just a few minutes chopping and then let the oven do the work for you. Serve with some tomato chutney.

1 Preheat the oven to 220°C (200°C fan oven) mark 7. Put the potatoes in a roasting tin – they should sit in one layer. Drizzle over the oil and season with salt and freshly ground black pepper. Toss well to coat the potatoes in oil, then put the rosemary on top (if using) and roast in the oven for 20 minutes.

2 Remove the roasting tin from the oven and add the onion wedges. Toss again to coat the onions and turn the potatoes. Put the sausages in between the potatoes and onions. Return the tin to the oven for 50 minutes–1 hour.

Spicy bean and sausage casserole

PREPARATION TIME: 10 minutes
COOKING TIME: 50 minutes
PER SERVING: 400cals, 18g fat, 38g carbohydrate

SERVES 4

6 chorizo sausages – around 50g (2oz) each
1 onion, chopped
2 garlic cloves, crushed
1 red pepper, deseeded and cut into strips
1 level tsp smoked Spanish paprika
1tsp red wine vinegar
400g can chopped tomatoes
4 sundried tomatoes, drained from oil and chopped
1 level tbsp tomato paste
1 level tbsp treacle
1 level tbsp dark muscovado sugar
1 bay leaf
435g can pinto beans, drained
4 level tbsp breadcrumbs
2 level tbsp chopped fresh parsley

Use smoked paprika in this dish rather than the regular variety as it adds a subtle flavour that works really well with the chorizo sausage.

1 Heat a 2.5 litre (4¼–4½ pint) flameproof casserole dish for 2–3 minutes, add the chorizo sausages, and cook until lightly browned. Add the onion, garlic and pepper, then fry until softened and golden. Add the smoked paprika and red wine vinegar, then stir well and cook for 30 seconds.

2 Add the tomatoes, sundried tomatoes, tomato paste, treacle, sugar and bay leaf, and season with salt and freshly ground black pepper. Bring to the boil, cover and simmer gently for 20 minutes.

3 Add the beans, cover and cook for 10 minutes. Preheat the grill. Uncover the casserole, sprinkle the breadcrumbs and parsley over and grill for 2–3 minutes until the breadcrumbs are crisp and golden, then serve.

Chorizo sausage and potato pan-fry

PREPARATION TIME: 10 minutes
COOKING TIME: 30 minutes
PER SERVING: 430cals, 24g fat, 30g carbohydrate

SERVES 4

2tbsp olive oil

450g (1lb) potatoes, cut into 2.5cm (1in) cubes

2 red onions, sliced

1 red pepper, deseeded and diced

1 level tsp paprika

300g (11oz) piece of chorizo sausage, skinned and cut
    into chunky slices

250g pack cherry tomatoes

100ml (3½fl oz) dry sherry

2tbsp chopped fresh flat-leafed parsley

Look out for the large, spicy, cured Spanish sausage known as chorizo at or around the supermarket deli counters – it has a fabulous smoked flavour and combines well with crispy paprika potatoes and sweet juicy cherry tomatoes. *Illustrated*

1 Heat the oil in a large, heavy-based frying pan. Add the potatoes and fry for 7–10 minutes until lightly browned, turning regularly.

2 Reduce the heat, add the onions and red pepper and continue to cook for 10 minutes, stirring from time to time until they have softened but not browned.

3 Add the paprika and chorizo sausage and cook for 5 minutes, stirring from time to time.

4 Add the cherry tomatoes and pour in the dry sherry. Stir everything together and cook for 5 minutes, until the sherry has reduced down and the tomatoes have softened and warmed through.

5 Sprinkle the chopped parsley over the top and serve.

Chorizo sausage and chickpea stew

PREPARATION TIME: 10 minutes
COOKING TIME: 15 minutes
PER SERVING: 540cals, 30g fat, 38g carbohydrate

SERVES 4

2tbsp olive oil

2 small onions, sliced

2 garlic cloves, chopped

1 level tsp smoked Spanish paprika

6 chorizo sausages, sliced

400g can chopped tomatoes

2 x 410g cans chickpeas, drained

2tbsp dry sherry

5 level tbsp chopped fresh flat-leafed parsley

The chorizo sausages combine well with the nuttiness of the chickpeas to add lots of flavour to this warming stew.

1 Heat the oil in a large frying pan, add the onions and garlic and fry gently for 5 minutes.

2 Stir in the paprika and cook for 30 seconds, then stir in the sliced chorizo. Fry for 2–3 minutes, then pour in the tomatoes and chickpeas.

3 Increase the heat and cook for 5 minutes or until warmed. Splash in the sherry and cook for 1 minute. Add the parsley and season with freshly ground black pepper. Serve with green salad and crusty bread.

Pan-fried pork chops with lentils

PREPARATION TIME: 10 minutes
COOKING TIME: 55 minutes
PER SERVING: 640cals, 31g fat, 40g carbohydrate

SERVES 4

2tbsp olive oil

4 x 175g (6oz) pork loin chops with bone

125g (4oz) lardons or bacon pieces

1 medium onion, chopped

2 garlic cloves, finely chopped

250g (9oz) small green lentils, such as Puy lentils, rinsed

200g (7oz) can chopped tomatoes

900ml (1½ pints) stock

2tbsp chopped fresh parsley

Lentils, low in fat and high in protein and fibre, have a mild, earthy flavour. Puy lentils take a little longer to cook than ordinary lentils but hold their shape well.

1 Heat the olive oil in a large frying or sauté pan. Add the pork chops and brown well on both sides, then remove from the pan. Add the lardons or bacon and cook until the fat runs, then drain away the fat, leaving about 1tbsp.

2 Add the onion and garlic and cook until softened. Add the lentils and tomatoes and stir well. Pour the stock over, bring to the boil and cook for 10 minutes, then reduce to a simmer. Put the pork chops on top, cover and cook for 35 minutes, adding more stock if necessary during cooking.

3 Season to taste with salt and freshly ground black pepper. Transfer the pork chops to warmed plates, stir the parsley into the cooked lentils and serve with the pork.

Pork chops with mustard sauce

PREPARATION TIME: 15 minutes
COOKING TIME: 30 minutes
PER SERVING: 400cals, 23g fat, 21g carbohydrate

SERVES 6

25g (1oz) butter

6 spare-rib pork chops, trimmed of fat

700g (1½lb) onions, chopped

700g (1½lb) trimmed leeks, chopped

1 garlic clove, crushed

900ml (1½ pints) milk

1 bay leaf

Fresh thyme sprig

120ml (4fl oz) double cream or crème fraîche

3 level tbsp made English mustard

Use spare-rib chops as loin chops won't be tender enough for this recipe.

1 Heat the butter in a flameproof casserole. When foaming, fry the chops briskly until very light golden brown then put to one side. Add the onions and leeks and cook gently until soft; add the garlic and cook for 30 seconds.

2 Pour in the milk and bring to the boil. Replace the chops, add the herbs and bubble gently for 10 minutes. When the pork is tender, put on to serving plates and keep warm.

3 Bubble the sauce until reduced almost to nothing then add the cream or crème fraîche and mustard, season well with salt and freshly ground black pepper and pour over the chops to serve.

Honey pork with roast potatoes and apples

PREPARATION TIME: 20 minutes
COOKING TIME: 1 hour 45 minutes
PER SERVING: 770cals, 34g fat, 45g carbohydrate

SERVES 4

1kg (2¼lb) loin of pork, with crackling and 4 bones

1 level tsp salt

4tbsp olive oil

25g (1oz) butter

700g (1½lb) Charlotte potatoes, scrubbed and halved
 lengthways

1 large onion, cut into eight wedges

1 level tbsp clear honey mixed together with 1 level tbsp
 grainy mustard

2 Cox apples, cored and each cut into six wedges

12 sage leaves

175ml (6fl oz) dry cider

For really crisp crackling, leave the joint uncovered in the fridge overnight to dry out the skin, then score the fat with a clean Stanley knife and rub with a little oil and salt. Buy a 100g bag of bistro salad, put in a large bowl, drizzle with 1tbsp balsamic vinegar and serve with the roast pork to cut through the richness.

1 Preheat the oven to 240°C (220°C fan oven) mark 9. Put the pork on a board and use a clean Stanley knife to score the skin into thin strips, cutting about halfway into the fat underneath. Rub the salt and 2tbsp of the oil over the skin and season well with freshly ground black pepper.

2 Put the meat on a rack, skin-side up, over a large roasting tin. (If you don't have a rack, just put the pork in the tin.) Roast in the oven on a high shelf for 25 minutes. Turn the oven down to 190°C (170°C fan oven) mark 5 and continue to roast for 15 minutes.

3 Add the remaining oil and the butter to the roasting tin. Scatter the potatoes and onion around the meat, season with salt and freshly ground black pepper and continue to roast for 45 minutes.

4 Brush the meat with the honey and mustard mixture. Add the apples and sage leaves to the tin and roast for a further 15 minutes.

5 Remove the pork from the tin and wrap completely with foil, then leave to rest. Put the potatoes, onions and apples in a serving dish and put back in the oven to keep warm.

6 Put the roasting tin on the hob and heat, then add the cider and stir well to make a thin gravy. Season with salt and freshly ground black pepper.

7 Cut the meat away from the bone. Cut between each bone. Pull the crackling away from the meat and cut into strips. Carve the joint, giving each person some meat, crackling and a bone to chew, and serve with the gravy and potatoes, onion and apples.

Roasted parsnips with leeks, apple and bacon

PREPARATION TIME: 10 minutes

COOKING TIME: 30 minutes

PER SERVING: 500cals, 41g fat, 23g carbohydrate

SERVES 2

2 parsnips, peeled and cut into six lengthways

175g pack baby leeks, trimmed and cut in half crosswise

2 medium red apples, unpeeled and cored, each cut into six wedges

50g (2oz) butter, diced

4 rashers rindless streaky bacon

Roasting vegetables is a breeze – once you've prepared them, the oven does all the work. These are cooked in butter to give them a richer, rounder flavour. *Illustrated*

1 Preheat the oven to 220°C (200°C fan oven) mark 7.
2 Put the parsnips, leeks and apples in a single layer in a roasting tin and dot the diced butter over them.
3 Lay the rashers of streaky bacon on top of the vegetables, put in the oven and roast for around 25 minutes, or until parsnips are soft and the bacon is crisp.

Pork tenderloin with creamy mustard sauce

PREPARATION TIME: 10 minutes

COOKING TIME: 30 minutes

PER SERVING: 290cals, 12.8g fat, 10.2g carbohydrate

SERVES 4

1 tbsp groundnut oil

500g (1lb 2oz) pork tenderloin, cut into 2cm (¾in) slices

7g (¼oz) butter

1 onion, finely chopped

1 small, red-skinned eating apple, cored and cut into eight wedges, then tossed in the juice of ½ lemon

1 level tsp light muscovado sugar

100ml (3½fl oz) each dry cider and chicken stock

100ml (3½fl oz) half-fat crème fraîche

1 level tsp wholegrain Dijon mustard

1 level tbsp chopped fresh tarragon

This sauce is so lovely and rich you'd never believe how few calories the dish has.

1 Heat the oil in a non-stick frying pan and cook the tenderloin slices in two batches over a high heat for 5 minutes or until golden all over. Put to one side.
2 Add butter to the pan, add the onion and cook for 1–2 minutes. Add the apple with any lemon juice and sauté over a medium heat for 5 minutes. Turn up the heat, add the sugar and stir-fry until everything is just golden – about 3 minutes.
3 Add the cider and bring to the boil. Add the stock and return the meat to the pan. Lower the heat and simmer, uncovered, for 1–2 minutes. Add the crème fraîche, mustard and tarragon, season with salt and freshly ground black pepper and cook for 1–2 minutes until the sauce is heated through, then serve.

Braised lamb shanks with cannellini beans

PREPARATION TIME: 15 minutes

COOKING TIME: 3 hours

PER SERVING: 490cals, 25g fat, 20g carbohydrate

SERVES 6

3tbsp olive oil

6 lamb shanks, trimmed

1 large onion, chopped

3 carrots, sliced

3 sticks celery, sliced

2 garlic cloves, crushed

2 x 400g cans chopped tomatoes

150ml (¼ pint) balsamic vinegar

2 bay leaves

2 x 410g cans cannellini beans, drained and rinsed

Lamb shanks are great for slow cooking – the meat becomes meltingly tender, falling off the bone. The vegetables cook down to a rich sauce, given extra flavour with balsamic vinegar. Serve with some crusty bread – ciabatta would be perfect. *Illustrated*

1 Preheat the oven to 170°C (150°C fan oven) mark 3. Heat the oil in a large ovenproof casserole. Add the lamb shanks in batches and brown all over. Remove from the pan and set aside.

2 Add the onion, carrots, celery and garlic to the pan and cook gently until just beginning to colour. Return the lamb to the pan and add the tomatoes and balsamic vinegar, giving the mixture a good stir. Season with salt and freshly ground black pepper and add the bay leaves. Bring to the boil, cover, and cook for 5 minutes on the hob, then transfer to the oven for 1½–2 hours, or until the shanks are nearly tender.

3 Remove the dish from the oven and add the beans. Cover and put back in the oven for a further 30 minutes, then serve.

Luxury lamb and leek hot pot

PREPARATION TIME: 20 minutes

COOKING TIME: 2 hours 50 minutes

PER SERVING: 530cals, 33g fat, 27g carbohydrate

SERVES 6

50g (2oz) butter

400g (14oz) leeks, trimmed and sliced

1 medium onion, chopped

1tbsp olive oil

800g (1lb 12oz) casserole lamb, cubed and tossed with
   1 level tbsp plain flour

2 garlic cloves, crushed

800g (1lb 12oz) waxy potatoes, such as Desirée, peeled
   and sliced

3 level tbsp chopped fresh parsley

1 level tsp chopped fresh thyme

300ml (½ pint) lamb stock

142ml carton double cream

Juices from the lamb and leeks mingle with the potatoes, stock and cream, giving this dish a wonderful rounded flavour.

1 Melt half the butter in a 3.5 litre (6¼ pint) flameproof casserole dish. Add the leeks and onion, stir to coat, then cover and cook over a low heat for 10 minutes.

2 Lift the leeks and onions out on to a large sheet of greaseproof paper. Add the oil to the casserole and heat, then brown the meat in batches with the garlic and plenty of salt and freshly ground black pepper. Remove and set aside on another large sheet of greaseproof paper.

3 Preheat the oven to 170°C (150°C fan oven) mark 3. Put half the potatoes in a layer over the bottom of the casserole and season with salt and freshly ground black pepper. Add the meat, then spoon the leek mixture on top. Arrange a layer of overlapping potatoes on top of that, sprinkle with herbs, then pour in the stock.

4 Bring the casserole to the boil, cover, then cook on a low shelf in the oven for about 1 hour 50 minutes. Remove the lid, dot with the rest of the butter and add the cream. Cook uncovered for 30–40 minutes until the potatoes are golden brown.

Lamb with spiced aubergine and spinach

PREPARATION TIME: 20 minutes
COOKING TIME: 20 minutes
PER SERVING: 381cals, 24g fat, 10g carbohydrate

SERVES 2

2tbsp olive oil

1 aubergine, sliced lengthways into 5mm (¼in) pieces

Pinch of crushed chillies

1 level tsp each ground cumin and coriander seeds

1 rack of lamb, around 6 bones, trimmed and sliced into cutlets

75g (3oz) baby leaf spinach

125g (4oz) cucumber, diced

10 mint leaves, roughly torn if large

6tbsp natural low-fat yogurt

Juice of ½ lemon

1 garlic clove, crushed

This is a very healthy dish – aubergine is rich in antioxidants, which help prevent heart disease and cancer, while spinach contains iron, and yogurt is a source of calcium. *Illustrated*

1 Preheat the oven to 110°C (fan oven 90°C) mark ¼. Brush a little oil over each side of the aubergine slices and sprinkle with the spices.
2 Heat a non-stick griddle pan, then fry the aubergine on each side for 4—5 minutes. Put in the oven and keep warm.
3 Wipe out the griddle pan and heat. Brush each side of the lamb cutlets with the remaining oil and pan-fry for 2—3 minutes on each side until still pink in the middle.
4 Put the spinach, cucumber and mint in a bowl and toss. Mix the yogurt, lemon and garlic and serve with the lamb, aubergine and spinach salad.

One-pot roast lamb with smoky bacon pasta

PREPARATION TIME: 5 minutes
COOKING TIME: 1 hour
PER SERVING: 500cals, 30g fat, 22g carbohydrate

SERVES 4

1 mini boneless leg of lamb roasting joint – about 450g (1lb) total weight

125g (4oz) smoked bacon lardons

150ml (¼ pint) red wine

300–350g carton or jar tomato pasta sauce with chilli

300ml (½ pint) hot chicken stock

75g (3oz) dried pasta shapes, such as penne

4 sundried tomatoes, drained of oil and cut into strips

1 level tbsp capers, rinsed

1 level tsp golden caster sugar (optional)

150g (5oz) chargrilled artichokes in oil, drained

Fresh flat-leafed parsley to garnish

Small boneless lamb roasts are good value and cook in an hour. Served like this with pasta it will make a hearty supper for four.

1 Preheat the oven to 200°C (180°C fan oven) mark 6. Put the lamb and lardons in a small deep roasting tin just large enough to hold the lamb. Fry for 5 minutes or until the lamb is brown all over and the lardons are beginning to crisp.
2 Remove the lamb and put to one side. Stir the wine into the tin (it should bubble immediately). Scrape the tin to loosen any crusty bits then bubble the wine until half has evaporated. Stir in all the other ingredients except the artichokes.
3 Put the lamb on a rack over the roasting tin so the meat juices drip into the pasta. Put in the oven, uncovered, and cook for about 50 minutes. The high temperature keeps the liquid bubbling and cooks the pasta. If the sauce reduces too much, stir in a little extra stock or water. Stir in the drained artichokes 5 minutes before the end of the cooking time.
4 To serve, slice the lamb and serve on top of the pasta, garnished with the parsley.

5

RICE DISHES

SALMON KEDGEREE

CURRIED COCONUT VEGETABLE RICE

MUSSEL AND SAFFRON PILAFF

RED RICE, SPINACH AND BEAN PILAFF

SMOKED SAUSAGE AND PRAWN JAMBALAYA

ITALIAN RISOTTO

SPINACH RISOTTO

PUMPKIN RISOTTO WITH HAZELNUT BUTTER

PORK, GARLIC AND BASIL RISOTTO

VEGETABLE AND SAFFRON RISOTTO

Salmon kedgeree

PREPARATION TIME: 15 minutes, plus 15 minutes soaking
COOKING TIME: 55 minutes
PER SERVING: 540cals, 21g fat, 62g carbohydrate

SERVES 4

50g (2oz) butter
700g (1½lb) onions, sliced
2 level tsp garam masala
1 garlic clove, crushed
75g (3oz) split green lentils, soaked in 300ml (½ pint)
    boiling water for 15 minutes, then drained
750ml (1¼ pints) hot vegetable stock
225g (8oz) basmati rice
1 green chilli, deseeded and finely chopped
350g (12oz) salmon fillet
Coriander sprigs to garnish

This was originally a dish associated with the British raj, although a vegetarian version was popular in India before their arrival. Often omitted from modern versions, the lentils add an authentic taste. This is an adaptation of the original and uses salmon instead of the more common smoked haddock. For a hotter flavour use a red chilli instead of green.

1 Melt the butter in a flameproof casserole. Add the onions and cook for 5 minutes or until soft. Remove a third and put to one side. Increase the heat and cook the remaining onions for 10 minutes to caramelise. Remove and put to one side.

2 Return the first batch of onions to the casserole, add the garam masala and garlic and cook, stirring, for 1 minute. Add the drained lentils and stock, cover and cook for 15 minutes. Add the rice and chilli, season, bring to the boil, cover and simmer for 5 minutes.

3 Put the salmon fillet on top of the rice, cover and continue to cook gently for 15 minutes or until the rice is cooked, the stock absorbed and the salmon opaque.

4 Lift off the salmon and divide into flakes. Return the salmon to the casserole and fork through the rice. Garnish with the reserved caramelised onions and the coriander sprigs and serve.

Curried coconut vegetable rice

PREPARATION TIME: 20 minutes
COOKING TIME: 35 minutes, plus 5 minutes standing
PER SERVING: 540cals, 28g fat, 63g carbohydrate

SERVES 6

100ml (3½fl oz) vegetable oil
1 large onion, chopped
1 level tbsp black mustard seeds
3 level tbsp korma curry paste
1 large aubergine – about 300g (11oz) – cut into 2cm (¾in) cubes
1 large butternut squash – about 500g (1lb 2oz) – peeled and cut into 2cm (¾in) cubes
250g (9oz) dwarf beans, trimmed and cut into 2cm (¾in) pieces
350g (12oz) basmati rice
2 level tsp salt
400ml can coconut milk
200g (7oz) baby spinach leaves

This colourful combination of butternut squash, aubergine, green beans and spinach, cooked with a spicy curry paste, coconut milk and rice, makes a perfect vegetarian main course.

1 Heat the vegetable oil in a large pan. Add the onion and cook for around 5 minutes, until light golden. Add the mustard seeds and cook, stirring, until they start to pop. Stir in the curry paste and cook for 1 minute.

2 Add the aubergine and cook, stirring, for 5 minutes. Add the butternut squash, beans, rice and the salt and mix well. Pour in the coconut milk and add 600ml (1 pint) of cold water. Bring to the boil, cover, and simmer for 15–18 minutes.

3 When the rice and vegetables are cooked, remove the lid and put the spinach on top. Cover and leave off the heat for 5 minutes. Gently stir the spinach through and serve immediately.

Mussel and saffron pilaff

PREPARATION TIME: 10 minutes, plus soaking
COOKING TIME: 40 minutes
PER SERVING: 400cals, 14g fat, 57g carbohydrate

SERVES 4

4tbsp oil
1 large onion, finely chopped
2 garlic cloves, crushed
225g (8oz) long-grain rice
600ml (1 pint) hot fish or vegetable stock
Large pinch of saffron, soaked in 6tbsp boiling water for 15 minutes
1 bay leaf
450g (1lb) cooked mussels in the shell (see above)
50g (2oz) dried currants

Sold as thin strands, saffron gives this dish a wonderful colour and a distinctive aroma. Most supermarkets sell ready-cooked mussels, usually in a herb- or wine-based sauce. *Illustrated*

1 Preheat the oven to 190°C (170°C fan oven) mark 5. Heat the oil in a flameproof casserole, add the onion and cook slowly for 7–10 minutes or until soft and golden. Add the garlic and cook for 30 seconds before adding the rice. Cook, stirring, for 1–2 minutes. Pour on the stock, then add the saffron and its soaking liquid. Add the bay leaf, season well with salt and freshly ground black pepper and bring to the boil.

2 Cover, put in the oven and cook for 15–20 minutes or until the rice is tender but still retains some bite.

3 Add the cooked mussels (with their sauce) and the currants to the casserole, cover and put back in the oven for 10 minutes or until the mussels are hot.

Red rice, spinach and bean pilaff

PREPARATION TIME: 15 minutes
COOKING TIME: 1½ hours
PER SERVING: 230cals, 6g fat, 36g carbohydrate

SERVES 4

2tbsp oil

225g (8oz) onions, chopped

2 garlic cloves, crushed

75g (3oz) each red rice and long-grain rice

450ml (¾ pint) vegetable or chicken stock

400g can beans, such as pinto, chickpeas, kidney beans
    or mixed pulses, drained and rinsed

225g (8oz) spinach, well washed, drained and roughly
    chopped

Red rice is a semi-wild variety with a pleasant, nutty flavour. This is a great dish for a chilly day.

1 Preheat the oven to 200°C (180°C fan oven) mark 6. Heat the oil in a large flameproof casserole, add the onions and cook, stirring, for 10 minutes or until they are golden and soft.

2 Add the garlic and the red rice to the onions; cook, stirring, for 1 minute. Add the stock, bring to the boil and season, then cover and simmer for 10 minutes.

3 Put in the oven and cook for 30 minutes. Add the long-grain rice to the casserole and bring back to the boil on the hob. Put back in the oven and cook for 25 minutes or until the rice is just tender.

4 Stir in the beans and put back in the oven for 5 minutes. Just before serving, stir the spinach through the pilaff until wilted. Season and serve.

Smoked sausage and prawn jambalaya

PREPARATION TIME: 15 minutes
COOKING TIME: 40 minutes
PER SERVING: 550cals, 25g fat, 59g carbohydrate

SERVES 4

2tbsp sunflower oil

175g (6oz) onion, finely chopped

6 baby red peppers, halved, or 2 large red peppers,
    roughly chopped

225g (8oz) long-grain and wild rice mix

750ml (1¼ pints) stock

5 level tbsp Creole sauce

150g (5oz) cooked, smoked pork sausages, sliced

125g (4oz) cooked and peeled king prawns

50g (2oz) shelled pistachio nuts

Large handful of fresh thyme sprigs and 4 lemon wedges
    to garnish

Next to pasta, rice has to be the most useful ingredient in the storecupboard. This delicious one-pot supper can be adapted, so you can use any leftover meat – from a Sunday joint, for instance – to replace the smoked pork sausage. *Illustrated*

1 Heat the oil in a large deep frying pan and fry the onions for about 10 minutes until they're very soft and golden brown. Add the peppers and fry for a further 2–3 minutes until they're just glazed in the oil and beginning to soften.

2 Stir in the rice and fry for about 1 minute before adding the stock and the Creole sauce. Stir well and bring to the boil.

3 Cover the pan with a lid or foil and simmer for 10–15 minutes or until all the liquid has been absorbed. Taste the rice to test if it's tender. If not, top up the pan with a little extra stock and simmer uncovered for a few more minutes.

4 Add the sausages and prawns and stir gently over a low heat for 3–4 minutes until heated through. Stir in the pistachio nuts. Garnish with the thyme sprigs and lemon wedges and serve immediately.

Risottos

DO'S AND DON'TS FOR THE PERFECT RISOTTO

- Always use risotto (such as arborio) rice: the grains are thicker and shorter than long-grain rice and have a high starch content. This means that they absorb more liquid slowly, producing a creamy-textured risotto.
- The traditional method is to add hot stock, ladle by ladle, to the risotto, allowing it to be absorbed by the rice after each addition. However, follow the individual recipes, as it also works if you add half, let that absorb and then add the remainder.
- The correct heat is vital. If the risotto gets too hot, the liquid evaporates too quickly and the rice won't cook evenly. If the heat is too low, the risotto will be gluey. Over a medium heat the rice should cook in about 25 minutes.
- Don't leave your risotto! Classic recipes suggest you stir constantly to loosen the rice from the bottom of the pan.
- The quantity of liquid given is an approximate amount – adjust it so that, when cooked, the rice is tender but firm to the bite, and creamily bound together, neither runny nor dry.

Italian risotto

PREPARATION TIME: 5 minutes
COOKING TIME: 40 minutes
PER SERVING: 600cals, 33g fat, 51g carbohydrate

SERVES 4

50g (2oz) butter
2 garlic cloves, crushed
225g (8oz) each onion, celery and mushrooms, chopped
225g (8oz) risotto (arborio) rice
175g (6oz) salami, chopped
150ml (¼ pint) white wine
450ml (¾ pint) hot chicken stock
1 level tbsp chopped chives
3 level tbsp freshly grated Parmesan cheese

Onions, celery, mushrooms and salami are the main ingredients here, whilst the wine added with the stock gives this risotto a special flavour. *Illustrated*

1 Melt the butter in a heavy-based pan. Add the garlic and onion and cook for 7–10 minutes until soft.
2 Add the celery and mushrooms and cook for 2–3 minutes. Stir in the rice, salami and wine and bring to the boil, stirring gently, until the wine is absorbed.
3 Over a medium heat, add the stock a little at a time, allowing all liquid to be absorbed after each addition. This should take about 20–25minutes. Stir in the chives and Parmesan, season and serve.

Spinach risotto

PREPARATION TIME: 10 minutes

COOKING TIME: 30 minutes

PER SERVING: 330cals, 10g fat, 50g carbohydrate

SERVES 4

25g (1oz) butter

1 onion, finely chopped

1 clove garlic, sliced

225g (8oz) risotto (arborio) rice

750ml (1¼ pints) hot vegetable stock

400g (14oz) fresh spinach, well washed and drained,
    tough stalks removed, and roughly chopped, or 125g
    (4oz) frozen leaf spinach

4 tbsp freshly grated Parmesan cheese, plus extra to serve

A risotto can't be rushed – the gradual addition of hot stock to the rice ensures that the rice is creamy and tender. The spinach gives this creamy risotto a lovely green colour; it's a real meal in itself. Try always to buy Parmesan cheese in a block; it's far superior to the ready-grated Parmesan sold in packs, which dries out and loses it flavour in the cupboard.

1 Gently heat the butter in a heavy-based nonstick pan. Add the onion and garlic and cook for about 5 minutes or until the onion is beginning to soften.

2 Add the rice to the pan, season and cook, stirring, for about 2–3 minutes. Add just enough stock to cover the rice and continue cooking, stirring all the time until most of the stock has been absorbed. Continue adding the stock in this way until it is completely absorbed and the rice is tender.

3 Squeeze the excess liquid from the frozen spinach, if using. Stir the fresh or frozen spinach into the rice. Heat through for 1–2 minutes or until the fresh spinach has just wilted.

4 Remove the pan from the heat and stir in the Parmesan cheese. Adjust the seasoning and serve immediately with a little extra grated Parmesan sprinkled on top.

Pumpkin risotto with hazelnut butter

PREPARATION TIME: 15 minutes
COOKING TIME: 40 minutes
PER SERVING: 660cals, 45g fat, 52g carbohydrate

SERVES 4

FOR THE BUTTER

50g (2oz) toasted hazelnuts, finely chopped
125g (4oz) softened butter
2 level tbsp chopped fresh parsley

FOR THE RISOTTO

50g (2oz) butter
175g (6oz) onion, finely chopped
900g (2lb) pumpkin, halved, peeled, deseeded and cut
  into small cubes
2 garlic cloves, crushed
225g (8oz) risotto (arborio) rice
600ml (1 pint) hot chicken stock
Zest of ½ orange
4tbsp freshly grated Parmesan cheese

For a quick supper, serve this risotto with a simple salad or, if you're entertaining, with grilled pork or escalopes. The hazelnut butter can be made in advance and frozen. If the pumpkin is unripe and very firm, you may need to increase the cooking time in step 3 to 8–10 minutes.

1 Put the hazelnuts, butter and parsley on to a piece of nonstick baking parchment. Season with freshly ground black pepper and mix together. Mould into a sausage shape, twist at both ends and chill.
2 To make the risotto, melt the butter in a large pan and fry the onion until soft but not brown. Add the pumpkin and sauté over a low heat for 5–8 minutes, until just beginning to soften.
3 Add the garlic and rice and stir until well mixed. Over a medium heat, add the stock a little at a time, allowing the liquid to be absorbed after each addition. This will take about 25 minutes.
4 Stir in the orange zest and Parmesan cheese and season. Serve the risotto with a slice of the hazelnut butter melting on top.

Pork, garlic and basil risotto

PREPARATION TIME: 15 minutes
COOKING TIME: 50 minutes
PER SERVING: 530cals, 24g fat, 36g carbohydrate

SERVES 6

6 thin escalopes pork, British veal or turkey
150g (5oz) Parma ham – about 6 slices
About 6 basil leaves
25g (1oz) plain white flour
About 65g (2½oz) unsalted butter
175g (6oz) onion, finely chopped
2 garlic cloves, crushed
225g (8oz) risotto (arborio) rice
450ml (¾ pint) white wine
450ml (¾ pint) hot chicken stock
3 level tbsp pesto sauce
50g (2oz) grated Parmesan cheese
4 level tbsp chopped fresh parsley

A simple tomato salad is the only accompaniment you will need for this creamy risotto.

1 Preheat the oven to 180°C (160°C fan oven) mark 4. If necessary, pound the escalopes carefully with a rolling pin until they are wafer-thin. Lay a slice of Parma ham on each escalope and put a basil leaf on top of the ham. Fix in place with a wooden cocktail stick. Season and dip in the flour, dusting off any excess.

2 Melt a small knob of the butter in a deep ovenproof pan and quickly fry the escalopes in batches for about 2–3 minutes on each side or until lightly golden. Melt a little more butter for each batch. You will need about half the butter at this stage. Remove and keep warm in the oven.

3 Melt about another 25g (1oz) of the butter in the pan and stir in the onion. Fry for about 10 minutes or until soft and golden. Add the garlic with the rice and stir well. Over a medium heat, add the wine and stock.

4 Bring to the boil then put in the oven and cook, uncovered, for 20 minutes.

5 Stir in the pesto, Parmesan cheese and parsley. Push the browned escalopes into the rice, cover and return the pan to the oven for a further 5 minutes or until the rice has completely absorbed the liquid and the escalopes are cooked through and piping hot.

Vegetable and saffron risotto

PREPARATION TIME: 15 minutes

COOKING TIME: 30 minutes

PER SERVING FOR 2: 570cals, 5g fat,
110g carbohydrate

PER SERVING FOR 4: 280cals 3g fat,
55g carbohydrate

**SERVES 2 AS A MAIN COURSE OR 4 AS AN
ACCOMPANIMENT**

1 tbsp olive oil

1 large courgette, chopped

1 each yellow and red pepper, deseeded and chopped

250g (9oz) risotto (arborio) rice

600ml (1 pint) vegetable stock

175g (6oz) flat mushrooms, chopped

Large pinch of saffron

1 bunch spring onions, trimmed and finely sliced

2 tomatoes, deseeded and chopped

Parmesan shavings, shredded fresh basil and basil leaves
    to garnish

Risotto always makes a great quick supper – this one is creamy and velvety, yet low in fat. Given the price of saffron, it's fortunate that a little goes a long way – it imparts both flavour and colour to a dish.

1 Heat the oil in a large, heavy-based pan, add the courgettes and fry for 2 minutes, then stir in the yellow and red peppers.

2 Add the rice, stir to coat in the oil then gradually add the stock, ladle by ladle, stirring as you go.

3 When the rice is tender – about 18–20 minutes – stir in the vegetables, the spring onions and tomatoes. Season generously with salt and freshly ground black pepper, garnish with the Parmesan, shredded basil and basil leaves and serve.

6

EGGS & CHEESE

EGG AND ROASTED PEPPER 'STEW'

SPINACH-BAKED EGGS WITH MUSHROOMS

SPEEDY POTATO AND CHORIZO TORTILLA

LAZY HAM AND CHEESE OMELETTE

COURGETTE AND PARMESAN FRITTATA

ARTICHOKE AND ROCKET FRITTATA

RED ONION TORTILLA

CHEAT'S GOAT'S CHEESE, SAUSAGE AND COURGETTE PIZZA

Egg and roasted pepper 'stew'

PREPARATION TIME: 15 minutes

COOKING TIME: 55 minutes

PER SERVING FOR 2: 600cals, 44g fat,
27g carbohydrate

PER SERVING FOR 3: 400cals, 30g fat,
18g carbohydrate

SERVES 2–3

4 tomatoes, preferably large plum, halved and deseeded

3 red peppers, halved, deseeded and chopped

225g (8oz) onions, preferably red, roughly sliced

1 red chilli

6 unpeeled garlic cloves

1 level tsp sugar

4tbsp olive oil

2 level tbsp sundried tomato paste

6 small eggs

Chopped fresh parsley or fried parsley to garnish

This is a colourful dish of eggs cooked in tomato shells, sitting on a bed of vegetables.

1 Preheat the oven to 230°C (210°C fan oven) mark 8. Roughly chop two tomato halves and put in one layer with the peppers in a roasting tin. Add the onions to the tin with the chilli and the garlic. Sprinkle with sugar, season well with salt and freshly ground black pepper and drizzle with the oil.

2 Put in the oven and cook for 25 minutes, stirring occasionally. Stir in the tomato paste. Sit the reserved tomato halves on top and cook for 20 minutes or until the peppers are charred.

3 Crack an egg into each tomato half, season well and spoon the pan juices over. Reduce the oven temperature to 180°C (160°C fan oven) mark 4. Return the tin to the oven for 7 minutes or until the eggs are just set. Garnish with the parsley and serve.

TO PREPARE AHEAD Complete the recipe to the end of step 2 up to one day ahead. Transfer to a non-metallic dish; cool and chill.

TO USE Reheat in an ovenproof dish, adding some oil if needed. Complete the recipe.

Spinach-baked eggs with mushrooms

PREPARATION TIME: 5 minutes
COOKING TIME: 13 minutes
PER SERVING: 440cals, 42g fat, 35g carbohydrate

SERVES 2

3tbsp olive oil
125g (4oz) closed-cup chestnut mushrooms, quartered
225g bag washed baby leaf spinach
2 large eggs
4tbsp double cream

The ultimate comfort food: an egg cooked until the white has set while the yolk is still soft and runny. Fresh spinach, mushrooms and thick cream add a touch of luxury to this simple dish.

1 Preheat the oven to 200°C (180°C fan oven) mark 6.
2 Heat the olive oil in a large frying pan, add the mushrooms and stir-fry for 30 seconds, then add the spinach and stir-fry until wilted. Season well with salt and freshly ground black pepper and divide between two 600ml (1 pint) ovenproof dishes.
3 Carefully break an egg into the centre of each dish and spoon the double cream over the top. Season well.
4 Cook for about 12 minutes, or until the eggs are just set. (Remember that they will continue to cook a little once they're out of the oven.) Serve immediately.

Speedy potato and chorizo tortilla

PREPARATION TIME: 10 minutes
COOKING TIME: 15 minutes
PER SERVING: 350cals, 20g fat, 25g carbohydrate

SERVES 4

1 tbsp olive oil
820g can new potatoes, drained and quartered
110g pack chorizo sausage, sliced
6 medium eggs, lightly beaten

You can't get much easier than this. No one will ever know you've used a can of potatoes – just make sure you hide the evidence. *Illustrated*

1 Preheat the grill. Heat the oil in a large frying pan and fry the potatoes until golden. Add the chorizo and cook for 1–2 minutes.
2 Add the eggs, season with salt and freshly ground black pepper and cook for 5 minutes over a low heat until golden underneath.
3 Put the pan under the grill for 1–2 minutes or until the eggs are just set. Serve immediately, cut into wedges.

Lazy ham and cheese omelette

PREPARATION TIME: 5 minutes
COOKING TIME: 30 minutes
PER SERVING: 400cals, 23g fat, 19g carbohydrate

SERVES 4

400g packet long-life sliced potato

125g (4oz) young spinach or watercress, well washed and
    drained

4 large eggs

150ml (¼ pint) milk

150g (5oz) mature Cheddar cheese, grated

150g (5oz) wafer-thin smoked ham

A simple dish to rustle up when you don't feel like cooking, this
omelette is packed with flavour.

1 Put the potato in a large nonstick frying pan and fry gently for about
20 minutes or until the potato is beginning to turn golden brown.

2 Add the spinach or watercress and cook for about 2 minutes or until it
starts to wilt.

3 Whisk together the eggs, milk and Cheddar cheese. Put the ham on
top of the spinach or watercress and potatoes and pour over the egg
mixture. Season with freshly ground black pepper and cook over a low
heat for about 5 minutes or until the egg mixture has just set. Preheat the
grill.

4 Put under the hot grill for about 3–4 minutes or until the cheese is
bubbling and golden brown. Cut into wedges and serve immediately.

Courgette and Parmesan frittata

PREPARATION TIME: 10 minutes
COOKING TIME: 15 minutes
PER SERVING: 260cals, 20g fat, 4g carbohydrate

SERVES 4

40g (1½ oz) butter

1 small onion, finely chopped

225g (8oz) courgettes, finely sliced

6 medium eggs, beaten

25g (1oz) freshly grated Parmesan cheese, plus shavings
    to garnish

Similar to the Spanish tortilla, the frittata is a thick, round
omelette that can have a wide choice of flavourings. *Illustrated*

1 Melt 25g (1oz) of the butter in an 18cm (7in) non-stick frying pan and
cook the onion until soft. Add the courgettes and fry gently for 5 minutes
or until they begin to soften.

2 Preheat the grill. Add the remaining butter to the frying pan. Season
the eggs with salt and freshly ground black pepper and pour into the
pan, cook for 2–3 minutes or until golden underneath and cooked round
the edges.

3 Scatter the grated cheese over the frittata and put under the preheated
grill for 1–2 minutes or until just set. Garnish with Parmesan shavings,
cut the frittata into quarters and serve with crusty bread.

Artichoke and rocket frittata

PREPARATION TIME: 10 minutes

COOKING TIME: 20 minutes

PER SERVING: 340cals, 27g fat, 5g carbohydrate

SERVES 4

3tbsp olive oil

1 medium onion, chopped

400g can artichoke hearts, drained, halved and patted
dry

10 large eggs, beaten

25g (1oz) fresh rocket leaves

If you're lucky enough to have access to a good Italian deli try buying some marinated baby artichokes for this recipe – they're delicious with eggs. *Illustrated*

1 Heat the oil in a 25.5cm (10in) diameter non-stick frying pan and gently fry the onion for about 10 minutes or until soft and translucent. Increase the heat and add the artichoke hearts. Cook on a low heat for 1–2 minutes or until lightly coloured.

2 Season the eggs with salt and freshly ground black pepper and mix in 4tbsp of cold water. Add to the artichoke mixture in the frying pan. Stir with a flat-edged wooden spoon, reducing the heat to allow the frittata to set gently. This should take about 7–8 minutes. Put under a hot grill for a few moments if you prefer your eggs well cooked.

3 Scatter the rocket leaves over the top and serve the frittata from the pan, cut into wedges.

Red onion tortilla

PREPARATION TIME: 5 minutes

COOKING TIME: 20 minutes

PER SERVING: 310cals, 26g fat, 5g carbohydrate

SERVES 6

50g (2oz) butter

2 tbsp olive oil

2 large red onions, finely sliced

4 level tbsp chopped fresh flat-leafed parsley

12 large eggs, lightly beaten

2 tbsp grated Parmesan cheese

An ideal Sunday supper – the red onions give the frittata a sweet, nutty flavour. Serve with a green salad.

1 Heat the butter and olive oil gently in a large frying pan. Add the onions and cook over a low heat until they're very soft and lightly caramelised.

2 Add the parsley, pour in the eggs and season with salt and freshly ground black pepper. Cook over a gentle heat, lifting the edges occasionally and tipping the egg around, until nearly cooked through. If you prefer your egg firm, put under a hot grill for about a minute. Sprinkle with the Parmesan cheese and serve.

Cheat's goat's cheese, sausage and courgette pizza

PREPARATION TIME: 15 minutes
COOKING TIME: 30 minutes
PER SERVING: 450cals, 21g fat, 49g carbohydrate

SERVES 4

2 x 20.5cm (8in) pizza bases
4 level tsp Dijon mustard
1 large red onion, thinly sliced
225g (8oz) courgettes, sliced wafer thin
2 spicy pepperoni sausages
2 x 100g (3½ oz) packets soft goat's cheese
Fresh thyme sprigs
Olive oil to drizzle

If you love homemade pizza but don't have time to make your own dough, use shop-bought pizza bases. They can be assembled in minutes, then left to cook while you get on with other things. *Illustrated*

1 Put two baking sheets in the oven and preheat to 200°C (180°C fan oven) mark 6.
2 Put the pizza bases on the baking sheets and spread with the mustard then sprinkle over the onion and courgette slices; season with salt and freshly ground black pepper.
3 Remove the sausages from their casing and crumble on top of each pizza with the soft goat's cheese. Sprinkle the thyme over and drizzle with olive oil.
4 Return to the oven and cook for 30 minutes or until the crust and sausage are brown and the vegetables are cooked. Swap the pizzas around in the oven halfway so they cook evenly.

7

VEGETARIAN DISHES

ROASTED VEGETABLE CROSTINI

CHILLI VEGETABLE AND COCONUT STIR-FRY

COURGETTE PUFF PIE

GARLIC CHEESE PIZZA

MAURITIAN VEGETABLE CURRY

PUMPKIN AND CHEESE BAKE

CHICKPEA STEW

WILD MUSHROOM SAUTÉ

SPICED BEAN AND VEGETABLE STEW

ROASTED RATATOUILLE

CRUSHED POTATOES WITH FETA AND OLIVES

Roasted vegetable crostini

PREPARATION TIME: 10 minutes

COOKING TIME: 30 minutes

PER SERVING: 260cals, 13g fat, 31g carbohydrate

SERVES 6

2 sweet romano peppers, deseeded and sliced

2 garlic cloves, peeled and sliced

300g pack cherry tomatoes on the vine, divided into
   six sprigs

1 red onion, sliced

5tbsp olive oil

1 sfilatino, ciabatta, or baguette, sliced

1tbsp balsamic vinegar

Few fresh basil leaves to garnish

These Italian toasts are perfect for lunch or as a snack.

1 Preheat the oven to 220°C (200°C fan oven) mark 7. Put the peppers, garlic, tomatoes and onion in a large roasting tin, drizzle with 2tbsp of the olive oil, season well with salt and freshly ground black pepper and cook for 30 minutes.

2 Halfway through cooking, drizzle the bread with 2tbsp of the oil and cook at the edge of the roasting tin for 15 minutes or until golden.

3 Top the bread with the roasted vegetables, drizzle with balsamic vinegar and the remaining olive oil and garnish with the basil.

Chilli vegetable and coconut stir-fry

PREPARATION TIME: 25 minutes
COOKING TIME: about 10 minutes
PER SERVING FOR 4: 290cals, 22g fat,
17g carbohydrate
PER SERVING FOR 6: 200cals, 15g fat,
11g carbohydrate

SERVES 4–6

2tbsp sesame oil

2 green chillies, deseeded and finely chopped

2.5cm (1in) piece fresh root ginger, finely grated

2 garlic cloves, crushed

1 level tbsp Thai green curry paste

125g (4oz) each carrot and mooli, cut into fine
  matchsticks

125g (4oz) baby sweetcorn, halved

125g (4oz) mangetout, halved on the diagonal

2 large red peppers, finely sliced

2 small pak choi, quartered

4 spring onions, finely chopped

300ml (½ pint) coconut milk

2 level tbsp peanut satay sauce

2tbsp soy sauce

1 level tsp soft brown sugar

4 level tbsp chopped fresh coriander

Whole roasted peanuts and fresh coriander sprigs
  to garnish

Mooli is also called daikon or white radish, and is popular in Asian cooking. Serve with prawn crackers.

1 Heat the oil in a wok or large non-stick frying pan and stir-fry the chilli, ginger and garlic for 1 minute. Add the curry paste and fry for a further 30 seconds.

2 Add the carrot, mooli, sweetcorn, mangetout and red pepper. Stir-fry over a fierce heat for 3–4 minutes then add the pak choi and spring onions. Cook, stirring, for a further 1–2 minutes.

3 Pour in the coconut milk, satay sauce, soy sauce and sugar. Season with freshly ground black pepper, bring to the boil and cook for 1–2 minutes, then add the coriander. Garnish with the peanuts and coriander sprigs and serve.

Courgette puff pie

PREPARATION TIME: 25 minutes, plus 10 minutes chilling
COOKING TIME: 40 minutes
PER SERVING: 650cals, 47g fat, 43g carbohydrate

SERVES 4

450g (1lb) courgettes
3tbsp olive oil
375g pack ready-rolled puff pastry
2 medium eggs
2 level tbsp crème fraîche
75g (3oz) Gruyère cheese, grated
2 garlic cloves, crushed
4 level tbsp chopped fresh parsley
50g (2oz) breadcrumbs

Shop-bought ready-made puff pastry is so good now that there's no need to make your own.

1 Preheat the oven to 200°C (180°C fan oven) mark 6. Put the courgettes on a large baking sheet and drizzle with the oil. Put in the oven and roast for 8 minutes.

2 Transfer the courgettes to a sheet of greaseproof paper and put the unwashed baking sheet to one side.

3 Roll out the pastry on a floured board until it measures 30.5cm (12in) square. Lift on to the baking sheet.

4 Crack one egg into a bowl and spoon in the crème fraîche, whisk lightly, then add 50g (2oz) of the cheese, along with the garlic and parsley. Season with salt and freshly ground black pepper and mix together until well combined.

5 Arrange the courgettes down the middle of the pastry and pour the egg and crème fraîche mixture over. Scatter the breadcrumbs and remaining cheese on top. Gather the pastry sides up and over the filling to create a thick pastry rim. Chill for 10 minutes.

6 Beat the remaining egg and brush over the pastry. Cook for 30 minutes or until the pastry is crisp and golden brown.

Garlic cheese pizza

PREPARATION TIME: 20 minutes
COOKING TIME: 30 minutes
PER SERVING: 700cals, 47g fat, 54g carbohydrate

SERVES 4

280g packet pizza-base mix
2 x 150g packs garlic and herb cream cheese
12 whole sundried tomatoes, drained from oil and cut into rough pieces
40g (1½ oz) pinenuts
12 fresh basil leaves
3tbsp olive oil

The combination of melting garlic cheese and tomatoes is heavenly on this quickly cooked pizza. For a deep and doughy base, use a packet of pizza-base mix.

1 Put a pizza stone or large baking sheet in the oven and preheat to 220°C (200°C fan oven) mark 7.

2 Mix the pizza-base dough according to the packet instructions. On a lightly floured surface, knead for a few minutes until smooth then roll out to a 33cm (13in) round. Transfer the dough to the preheated pizza stone or baking sheet. Pinch a lip around the edge.

3 Crumble the cheese over the dough and flatten with a palette knife. Then sprinkle on the sundried tomatoes, pinenuts and basil leaves.

4 Drizzle with the olive oil and cook for 20–30 minutes, or until pale golden and cooked to the centre.

Mauritian vegetable curry

PREPARATION TIME: 20 minutes
COOKING TIME: 30 minutes
PER SERVING: 190cals, 11g fat, 19g carbohydrate

SERVES 4

3tbsp vegetable oil

1 onion, finely sliced

4 cloves garlic, crushed

2.5cm (1in) piece root ginger, grated

3 level tbsp medium curry powder

6 fresh curry leaves

150g (5oz) potato, peeled and cut into 1cm (½in) cubes

125g (4oz) aubergine, cut into 2cm (1in) long sticks, 5mm (¼in) wide

150g (5oz) carrots, peeled and cut into 5mm (¼in) dice

900ml (1½ pints) vegetable stock

Pinch of saffron

1 level tsp salt

150g (5oz) green beans, trimmed

75g (3oz) frozen peas

3tbsp chopped fresh coriander

You'll find fresh curry leaves sold with fresh herbs in larger supermarkets. They give a lovely fragrance to this dish. Serve with some Indian bread such as naan, chapati or roti.

1 Heat the oil in a large heavy-based pan. Add the onion and fry over a gentle heat for 5–10 minutes until golden. Add the garlic, ginger, curry powder and curry leaves and fry for a further minute.

2 Add the potatoes and aubergines to the pan and fry, stirring, for 2 minutes. Add the carrots, stock, saffron, the salt and plenty of freshly ground black pepper. Cover and cook for 10 minutes until the vegetables are almost tender.

3 Add the beans and peas to the pan and cook for a further 4 minutes. Sprinkle with the chopped coriander and serve.

TO PREPARE AHEAD Complete the recipe to the end of step 2, add the beans and peas and chill immediately.

TO USE Put in a pan, cover and bring to the boil, then simmer for 10–15 minutes. Complete the recipe.

Pumpkin and cheese bake

PREPARATION TIME: 15 minutes
COOKING TIME: 50 minutes
PER SERVING: 660cals, 51g fat, 27g carbohydrate

SERVES 4

450g (1lb) new potatoes, halved
450g (1lb) pumpkin, peeled and thinly sliced
1 large onion – about 175g (6oz) – finely sliced
225g (8oz) buttery cheese, eg Taleggio, Gruyère or
    Fontina, thinly sliced
300ml (½ pint) crème fraîche

Few will be able to resist this dish of potatoes, pumpkin and cheese cooked in rich crème fraîche. With its crisp golden edges and melting sauce, it's good served with a baguette and green salad.

1 Preheat the oven to 220°C (200°C fan oven) mark 7. Boil the potatoes, pumpkin and onion together in salted water in a shallow flameproof casserole for 3–4 minutes. Drain off all the liquid and roughly mix in the cheese.

2 Beat a little cold water into the crème frâiche to give a thick pouring consistency. Season with freshly ground black pepper, then pour over the vegetables. Put the casserole on the hob and bring to the boil.

3 Transfer to the oven and cook, uncovered, for 40 minutes or until bubbling and golden. Two or three times during the cooking time, stir the crust that forms on top into the dish to add to the flavour. To check the dish is cooked, press the tip of a knife into the centre of a potato, which should be tender.

TO PREPARE AHEAD Complete the recipe, reserving a little of the crème fraîche mixture. Cool, cover and chill overnight.
TO USE Brush on the reserved crème fraîche, then reheat at 220°C (200°C fan oven) mark 7 for 15–20 minutes. If the top is very well browned, cover with foil while reheating, then crisp under a hot grill for 2–3 minutes.

Chickpea stew

PREPARATION TIME: 10 minutes

COOKING TIME: 40 minutes

PER SERVING: 210cals, 10g fat, 24g carbohydrate

SERVES 4

1 red, 1 green and 1 yellow pepper, each halved and
   deseeded

2tbsp olive oil

1 onion, finely sliced

2 cloves garlic, crushed

1 level tbsp harissa paste

2 level tbsp tomato paste

½ level tsp ground cumin

1 aubergine, diced

410g can chickpeas, drained and rinsed

450ml (¾ pint) vegetable stock

4 level tbsp roughly chopped fresh flat-leafed parsley

There's no need to splash out on loads of different spices to create this authentic Moroccan chickpea stew – buy a pot of harissa paste, which has a hot chilli flavour, for an instant boost. This stew, which is also suitable for vegans, actually improves in flavour if made 24 hours before you plan to eat it. Serve with couscous.

1 Preheat the grill and lay the peppers skin-side up on a baking sheet. Grill for around 5 minutes or until the skin begins to blister and char. Put the peppers in a plastic bag, seal and put to one side for a few minutes. When cooled a little, peel the skins and discard, then slice the peppers and put to one side.

2 Heat the oil in a large frying pan, add the onion and cook for 5–10 minutes or until softened. Add the garlic, harissa, tomato paste and cumin and cook for 2 minutes.

3 Add the peppers to the pan with the aubergine. Stir everything to coat evenly with the spices and cook for 2 minutes. Add the chickpeas and stock, season well with salt and freshly ground black pepper and bring to the boil. Simmer for 20 minutes.

4 Stir the parsley through the chickpea stew and serve.

Wild mushroom sauté

PREPARATION TIME: 10 minutes
COOKING TIME: 5 minutes
PER SERVING: 130cals, 14g fat, trace carbohydrate

SERVES 4

4 tbsp olive oil
2 garlic cloves, crushed
1 medium-sized red chilli, deseeded and finely sliced
450g (1lb) assorted wild mushrooms, roughly chopped
Juice of ½ lemon
1 tbsp fresh flat-leafed parsley

Serve as a first course with crisp, warm country-style bread.
Illustrated

1 Heat the olive oil in a large frying pan. Add the garlic and cook for 1 minute or until golden. Then add the sliced red chilli and cook for a further minute.
2 Add the mushrooms to the pan and cook over a brisk heat until all the liquid has evaporated.
3 Add the lemon juice and parsley. Season well with salt and freshly ground black pepper and serve immediately.

Spiced bean and vegetable stew

PREPARATION TIME: 20 minutes
COOKING TIME: 35 minutes
PER SERVING: 250cals, 8g fat, 42g carbohydrate

SERVES 6

3tbsp olive oil
2 small onions, sliced
2 garlic cloves, crushed
1 level tbsp sweet paprika
1 small dried red chilli, deseeded and finely chopped
700g (1½ lb) sweet potatoes, peeled and cubed
700g (1½ lb) pumpkin, peeled and cut into chunks
125g (4oz) okra, trimmed
500g jar passata
400g can haricot or cannellini beans, drained

This tasty stew features three of the more unusual vegetables – sweet potato, pumpkin and okra, but all are widely available in large supermarkets.

1 Heat the oil in a large heavy-based pan, add the onions and garlic and cook over a very gentle heat for 5 minutes.
2 Stir in the paprika and chilli and cook for 2 minutes, then add the sweet potatoes, pumpkin, okra, passata and 900ml (1½ pints) of cold water. Season generously with salt and freshly ground black pepper.
3 Cover the pan, bring to the boil and simmer for 20 minutes until the vegetables are tender. Add the beans, cook for 3 minutes to warm them through, then serve.

Roasted ratatouille

PREPARATION TIME: 15 minutes

COOKING TIME: 1½ hours

PER SERVING: 270cals, 23g fat, 14g carbohydrate

SERVES 6

400g (14oz) red peppers, deseeded and roughly
    chopped

700g (1½ lb) aubergines, stalk removed and cut into
    chunks

450g (1lb) onions, peeled and cut into petals

4–5 garlic cloves

150ml (¼ pint) olive oil

1 level tsp fennel seeds

200ml (7fl oz) passata

Few fresh thyme sprigs to garnish

Equally good cold, this dish is wonderful in the summer when peppers and aubergines are at their best.

1 Preheat the oven to 240°C (220°C fan oven) mark 9. Put the peppers, aubergines, onions, garlic, olive oil and fennel seeds in a roasting tin, then season with sea salt flakes and freshly ground black pepper and toss together.

2 Transfer to the oven and cook for 30 minutes, tossing frequently during cooking, or until the vegetables are charred and beginning to soften.

3 Stir the passata through the vegetables and return the roasting tin to the oven for 50–60 minutes, stirring occasionally. Garnish with the thyme sprigs and serve.

TO PREPARE AHEAD Complete the recipe to the end of step 1, cool, cover and chill overnight.

TO USE Complete the recipe.

TO FREEZE Complete the recipe to the end of step 1. Cool and put in a freezerproof container. Seal and freeze for up to three months.

TO USE Thaw at cool room temperature overnight. Complete the recipe.

Crushed potatoes with feta and olives

PREPARATION TIME: 5 minutes

COOKING TIME: 15 minutes

PER SERVING: 410cals, 29g fat, 29g carbohydrate

SERVES 4

700g (1½lb) new potatoes, unpeeled

75ml (3fl oz) olive oil

75g (3oz) pitted black olives, shredded

2 level tbsp chopped fresh flat-leafed parsley

200g (7oz) feta cheese, crumbled

Traditionally made from sheep's or goat's milk, feta is a white, crumbly cheese with a tangy flavour. The saltiness of the feta works well here with the new potatoes.

1 Cook the potatoes in their skins in a pan of boiling salted water for 15 minutes or until tender. Drain, put back in the pan and crush roughly with a fork.

2 Add the olive oil, olives, flat-leafed parsley and feta cheese. Season with freshly ground black pepper, toss together – don't over-mix or the potatoes will become glutinous – and serve.

8

PUDDINGS

COLD PUDDINGS

ICED COFFEE CUPS

RICH CHOCOLATE POTS

BOOZY ICE CREAM

SPICED CARAMELISED CLEMENTINES

GINGER AND MINT FRUIT SALAD

FIGS IN CINNAMON SYRUP

FRUIT BRÛLÉES

BANANA AND BERRY SMOOTHIE

ALMOND AND POLENTA CAKE

FRUITY RICE PUDDING

HOT PUDDINGS

ZABAGLIONE

PANETTONE CHOCOLATE BREAD AND BUTTER PUDDING

THE VERY BEST BREAD AND BUTTER PUDDING

GOLDEN CROISSANT PUDDING

RICE PUDDING

GINGER-GLAZED PINEAPPLE

BAKED PEARS WITH APRICOTS AND ALMONDS

LIME FRUITS

BANANAS GRILLED WITH CARDAMOM BUTTER

HOT FUDGE PEARS

CRUMBLY APPLE AND CHEESE CAKE

GOLDEN ORANGE SHORTCAKE

FOIL-BAKED FIGS WITH HONEY AND MARSALA

IMPRESS-YOUR-FRIENDS APPLE TART

Iced coffee cups

PREPARATION TIME: 5 minutes

FREEZING TIME: 2 hours plus 30 minutes fridge time

PER SERVING: 400cals, 35g fat, 19g carbohydrate

SERVES 6

350g (12oz) ricotta cheese

350g (12oz) mascarpone cheese

1tbsp rum

3tbsp coffee liqueur

1tbsp vanilla essence

2tbsp strong coffee

Dark chocolate shavings to serve

These darkly rich coffee cups make an ideal end to a special meal, yet are so simple to make.

1 Beat together the ricotta and mascarpone cheeses with the rum, coffee liqueur, vanilla essence and the coffee, until smooth and creamy.
2 Spoon into freezer-proof demi-tasse cups or small ramekins and freeze for at least 2 hours.
3 When ready to serve, transfer to the fridge for 30 minutes, sprinkle with dark chocolate shavings, then serve immediately. The mixture should be only just frozen.

Rich chocolate pots

PREPARATION TIME: 5 minutes

COOKING TIME: 10 minutes plus 20 minutes chilling

PER SERVING: 750cals, 64g fat, 38g carbohydrate

SERVES 6

200g bar dark chocolate, at room temperature

300g (11oz) dark chocolate, broken into squares

284ml carton double cream

250g tub mascarpone cheese

3tbsp cognac

1tbsp vanilla extract

6 level tbsp crème fraîche

Serve these luscious chocolate pots with *cigarettes russes* biscuits for their contrasting texture. *Illustrated*

1 Put the 200g bar of chocolate on a piece of greaseproof paper and scrape a very sharp chopping knife against it to make about 12 long, thin curls. Alternatively, drag a vegetable peeler across to create fine chocolate shavings.
2 Melt the dark chocolate in a bowl over a pan of simmering water. Take the bowl off the heat and add the cream, mascarpone, cognac and vanilla extract and mix well together – the hot chocolate will melt the cream and cheese.
3 Divide between six 150ml (¼ pint) glasses and chill for 20 minutes.
4 Spoon crème fraîche on top, decorate with the chocolate curls and serve.

Boozy ice cream

PREPARATION TIME: 5 minutes

COOKING TIME: 12 minutes

PER SERVING: 640cals, 53g fat, 27g carbohydrate

SERVES 4

284ml carton double cream

150ml (¼ pint) Baileys Original Irish Cream Liqueur

400g (14 oz) vanilla dairy ice cream

Chocolate-covered coffee beans, roughly chopped
    to serve

Totally wicked – yet so easy to achieve.

1 Heat the cream in a small pan and bubble for 10 minutes or until reduced by half, thick and syrupy.

2 Add the Baileys Original Irish Cream Liqueur and allow to bubble for 2 minutes, stirring occasionally.

3 Put three scoops of ice cream on each serving plate. Pour over the warm sauce and sprinkle with the coffee beans. Serve immediately.

Spiced caramelised clementines

PREPARATION TIME: 15 minutes

COOKING TIME: 25 minutes plus 4 hours chilling

PER SERVING: 130cals, 0g fat, 35g carbohydrate

SERVES 8

225g (8oz) golden caster sugar

2 cinnamon sticks, halved

15 cloves

2 star anise

Pared rind of 1 lemon

16 clementines or 8 satsumas, peeled and membrane
    removed

This dessert is best if it's made two or three days ahead. *Illustrated*

1 Heat the sugar with 300ml (½ pint) of cold water very slowly in a heavy-based pan until the sugar has dissolved, then bring to the boil and bubble until the syrup turns a dark caramel.

2 Remove from the heat and carefully add 300ml (½ pint) of warm water – it may splutter. Return to the heat to dissolve any hardened caramel.

3 Add the cinnamon sticks, cloves, star anise and lemon rind. Remove from the heat and allow to cool.

4 Slice each clementine or satsuma into five and spear with a cocktail stick to hold together. Put into a bowl, pour over the warm caramel and chill for at least 4 hours.

Ginger and mint fruit salad

PREPARATION TIME: 50 minutes, plus 30 minutes cooling and minimum 2 hours chilling
COOKING TIME: 30 minutes
PER SERVING: 205cals, 0g fat, 42g carbohydrate

SERVES 12

70cl bottle ginger wine
225g (8oz) golden caster sugar
25g (1oz) piece fresh ginger
3 large mangoes, peeled and roughly chopped
3 large papaya, peeled and roughly chopped
2 Charentais melons, peeled and roughly chopped
450g (1lb) seedless red grapes, removed from stalks
2 fresh mint sprigs, plus extra to decorate

This refreshing, summery fruit salad is best made the day before to allow the flavours to develop. You can buy ginger wine from most supermarkets and off-licences. These quantities are ideal for a buffet, but you can easily scale them down.

1 Put the wine, sugar and ginger in a pan with 600ml (1 pint) of cold water and heat gently until the sugar has dissolved. Increase the heat and bring to the boil, then turn down and simmer gently for 20–30 minutes. Leave to cool.
2 Put all the fruit in a large serving bowl and strain the cooled syrup over. Chill for at least 2 hours.
3 To serve, chop the mint leaves and add to the fruit salad. Decorate with mint sprigs.

TO PREPARE AHEAD Complete the recipe to the end of step 2, cover and chill for up to two days.
TO USE Complete the recipe.

Figs in cinnamon syrup

PREPARATION TIME: 15 minutes
COOKING TIME: 35 minutes, plus cooling and chilling
PER SERVING: 350cals, 0g fat, 74g carbohydrate

SERVES 4

1 orange
1 lemon
300ml (½ pint) red wine
50g (2oz) golden caster sugar
1 cinnamon stick
450g (1lb) ready-to-eat dried figs
Mascarpone cheese or ice cream to serve

These figs are delicious served warm or cold with mascarpone cheese or a good-quality vanilla ice cream. They can be kept, covered, in the fridge for up to one week. Just stir occasionally.

1 Pare the rind from the orange and lemon and put in a medium pan. Squeeze and add the orange and lemon juice with the wine, sugar and cinnamon stick. Bring very slowly to the boil, stirring occasionally.
2 Add the figs. Simmer very gently for 20 minutes until plump and soft. Remove the figs, rind and cinnamon with a slotted spoon and transfer to a serving bowl.
3 Return the liquid to the boil and bubble until syrupy, about 5 minutes. Pour over the figs, then cool, cover and chill.
4 If you like, warm the figs in the syrup for 3–4 minutes, then serve with mascarpone cheese or ice cream.

Fruit brûlées

PREPARATION TIME: 10 minutes
COOKING TIME: 10 minutes
PER SERVING: 110cals, 5g fat, 17g carbohydrate

SERVES 4

4 ripe nectarines or peaches, halved and stone removed
8tsp soft cream cheese
8tsp golden caster sugar

Cream cheese and fruit provide a perfect summer pudding in this easy dish.

1 Fill each stone cavity of the nectarines or peaches with 2 level tsp soft cream cheese and then sprinkle with 2 level tsp caster sugar.
2 Put on a grill pan and cook under a very hot grill until the sugar has browned and caramelised to create a brûlée crust. Serve warm.

Banana and berry smoothie

PREPARATION TIME: 10 minutes
PER SERVING: 70cals, trace fat, 15g carbohydrate

SERVES 6

2 large bananas – about 450g (1lb) – peeled and
    chopped
142ml carton natural yogurt
150ml (¼ pint) mineral water
500g bag frozen summer fruits

Wholesome, healthy and surprisingly filling, this smoothie is perfect for a healthy breakfast.

1 Put the bananas, yogurt and mineral water in a food processor and whiz until smooth.
2 Add the frozen berries and whiz until it creates a purée. If you prefer a really smooth texture, sieve the mixture using the back of a ladle to press it through. Serve in tall glasses.

Almond and polenta cake

PREPARATION TIME: 5 minutes
COOKING TIME: 40 minutes
PER SERVING: 580cals, 38g fat, 53g carbohydrate

SERVES 8

Butter to grease
225g (8oz) each golden caster sugar and ground
  almonds
225 (8oz) 'quick-cook' polenta
225g (8oz) butter, softened

Yellow polenta is coarsely ground maize that is usually cooked with water to a soft 'porridge' or a firm 'cake' and served as an accompaniment to savoury dishes. It can also be used to give a crumbly texture to bakes. 'Quick-cook' polenta, which is perfect for this recipe, is a pre-cooked, fine type of polenta available from delicatessens and major supermarkets. This cake will store well in an airtight container for up to three days. Serve, sliced, with a glass of chilled dessert wine or a cup of coffee.

1 Preheat the oven to 190°C (170°C fan oven) mark 5. Grease an 18cm (7in) loose-bottomed fluted flan tin with a little butter.
2 Mix all the dry ingredients together in a bowl and stir in the softened butter until it is well blended.
3 Press this mixture into the prepared flan tin, making sure that it is evenly spread.
4 Bake for 40 minutes or until golden brown and firm to the touch. Allow to cool in the tin before turning out to cool completely on a wire rack.

TO FREEZE Complete the recipe to the end of step 4. Cool and put in a freezerproof container. Seal and freeze for up to one month.
TO USE Thaw at cool room temperature for 2 hours.

Fruity rice pudding

PREPARATION TIME: 5 minutes
COOKING TIME: 1 hour plus 30 minutes cooling and minimum 1 hour chilling
PER SERVING: 390cals, 20g fat, 46g carbohydrate

SERVES 6

125g (4oz) pudding rice
1.1 litres (2 pints) full-fat milk
1tsp vanilla extract
3–4tbsp wild lingonberry sauce

The sharp lingonberry sauce contrasts wonderfully with the creamy rice in this pudding. You can buy lingonberry sauce in jars from some supermarkets or delicatessens. Alternatively, serve with raspberry or blackcurrant coulis, also sold in jars.

1 Put the rice in a pan with 600ml (1 pint) of cold water, bring to the boil and simmer until the liquid has evaporated. Add the milk, bring to the boil and simmer for 45 minutes or until the rice is very soft and creamy. Cool.
2 Add the vanilla extract and sugar to the rice. Chill for 1 hour.
3 Divide a third of the rice mixture between six glass tumblers, top with a spoonful of lingonberry sauce and repeat the process, finishing with the rice. Chill until ready to serve.

Zabaglione

PREPARATION TIME: 5 minutes
COOKING TIME: 20 minutes
PER SERVING: 270cals, 8g fat, 37g carbohydrate

SERVES 3 (OR 6 AS AN ACCOMPANIMENT)

4 medium egg yolks
100g (3½oz) golden caster sugar
100ml (4fl oz) sweet Marsala

This is heavenly served with Savoiardi biscuits.

1 Heat a pan of water to boiling point. Put the egg yolks and sugar into a heatproof bowl large enough to rest over the pan without touching the base. With the bowl in place, reduce the heat so that the water is just simmering.
2 Using a hand-held mixer, whisk the yolks and sugar for 15 minutes until pale, thick and foaming.
3 With the bowl still over the heat, gradually pour in the Marsala, whisking all the time.
4 Pour the zabaglione into glasses or small coffee cups and serve immediately.

Panettone chocolate bread and butter pudding

PREPARATION TIME: 30 minutes plus soaking plus 1 hour standing
COOKING TIME: 1–1¼ hours
PER SERVING: 720cals, 30g fat, 95g carbohydrate

SERVES 8

125g (4oz) raisins
110ml (4fl oz) brandy
2 x 500g cartons fresh custard, about 900ml (1½ pints) in
    total
568ml carton milk
Panettone, weighing about 700g (1lb 8oz), sliced into
    5mm (¼in) thick circles
75g (3oz) softened butter, plus extra to grease
200g (7oz) plain chocolate, roughly chopped
Icing sugar to dust

For an Italian variation on traditional bread and butter pudding, use panettone instead of bread. Panettone is a dome-shaped yeasted cake with sultanas, orange and citrus peel, sold in major supermarkets and delicatessens. This is one of Good Housekeeping's favourite winter puddings.

1 Soak the raisins in the brandy for at least 20 minutes. Stir the custard and milk together.
2 Spread the panettone slices with the softened butter and cut each circle into quarters. Grease a 3.4 litre (6 pint) ovenproof dish and pour a thin layer of custard over the base of the dish.
3 Layer the panettone, raisins, chocolate and custard in the dish, finishing with a layer of custard. Set aside and leave to soak for 1 hour.
4 Preheat the oven to 180°C (160°C fan oven) mark 4. Put the dish in a roasting tin and pour hot water around the dish to come halfway up the sides. Bake for 1–1¼ hours or until the custard is set and the top has turned a deep brown. Cover with foil after 40 minutes to prevent the top from burning, if necessary.
5 Dust the pudding lightly with icing sugar to serve.

TO FREEZE Complete the recipe to the end of step 3. Cool and put in a freezerproof container. Seal and freeze for up to one month.
TO USE Thaw overnight in the fridge, then complete the recipe.

The very best bread and butter pudding

PREPARATION TIME: 10 minutes, plus 10 minutes soaking
COOKING TIME: 30–40 minutes
PER SERVING: 480cals, 16g fat, 68g carbohydrate

SERVES 4

400g Irish Whiskey fruit loaf, cut into 1cm (½in) slices then diagonally in half again to make triangles
4 medium eggs
450ml (¾ pint) milk
3 level tbsp golden icing sugar

A variation on the traditional version, this bread and butter pudding uses fruit loaf flavoured with whiskey. *Illustrated*

1 Preheat the oven to 180°C (160°C fan oven) mark 4. Arrange the slices of fruit loaf in four 300ml (½ pint) gratin dishes or in one 1.1 litre (2 pint) dish.
2 Beat the eggs, milk and 2tbsp of the sugar in a bowl and pour over the fruit loaf. Soak for 10 minutes.
3 Put in the oven and bake for 30–40 minutes. Dust with the remaining icing sugar to serve.

Golden croissant pudding

PREPARATION TIME: 5 minutes
COOKING TIME: 50 minutes
PER SERVING FOR 4: 560cals, 40g fat, 38g carbohydrate
PER SERVING FOR 6: 370cals, 27g fat, 25g carbohydrate

SERVES 4–6

4 croissants or brioches, cut in half
50g (2oz) butter, softened
3 large eggs
300ml (½ pint) milk
284ml carton single cream
4 level tbsp golden syrup

This pudding is an excellent way to use up leftover croissants or brioches.

1 Preheat the oven to 150°C (130°C fan oven) mark 2. Spread the croissants or brioches with the butter. Mix together the eggs, milk and cream. Spoon 3 level tbsp of the golden syrup into a 1.4 litre (2½ pint) ovenproof dish.
2 Put the croissant or brioche halves in the dish and pour over the egg mixture. Then drizzle over the remaining golden syrup.
3 Put the dish in a roasting tin with enough hot water to come about halfway up the side. Put in the oven and bake for about 50 minutes or until lightly set. Serve hot.

Rice pudding

PREPARATION TIME: 5 minutes
COOKING TIME: 1½ hours
PER SERVING: 240cals, 7g fat,
36g carbohydrate

SERVES 6

A little butter to grease
125g (4oz) short-grain pudding rice
1.1 litre carton full-fat milk
4 level tbsp golden caster sugar
Zest of 1 small orange
2tsp vanilla extract
Whole nutmeg to grate

It takes just a couple of minutes to prepare this comforting pud, then it needs long slow cooking to complete. Orange zest is added for a fruity tang, but it's just as good without.

1 Preheat the oven to 180°C (160°C fan oven) mark 4. Lightly grease a 900ml (1½ pint) ovenproof dish. Add the pudding rice, milk, sugar, orange zest and vanilla extract and stir everything together. Grate the nutmeg all over the top of the mixture.

2 Bake the pudding in the oven for 1½ hours or until the top is golden brown, then serve.

Ginger-glazed pineapple

PREPARATION TIME: 30 minutes

COOKING TIME: 10 minutes

PER SERVING: 90cals, 0g fat, 24g carbohydrate

SERVES 8

2 medium-sized ripe pineapples, cut into four lengthways, with the stalk on

2 level tbsp light muscovado sugar

2 level tsp ground ginger

Yogurt to serve

1tsp runny honey (optional)

Ground ginger to dust

Ginger enhances the hot caramelised pineapple, giving it a subtle, fresh dimension.

1 Remove the fibrous core from each pineapple quarter and cut along the skin to loosen the flesh, reserving the skin 'shells'. Cut the flesh into pieces and put back in the pineapple 'shell'. Wrap the green leaves of the stalk in foil so that they don't burn while grilling. Mix the sugar and ground ginger together.

2 Preheat the grill. Sprinkle each pineapple quarter with the sugar mixture, put on foil-lined baking sheets and cook under the grill for 10 minutes or until golden and caramelised.

3 Mix the yogurt with the runny honey, if using. Serve the pineapple with the yogurt and dust with ginger.

Baked pears with apricots and almonds

PREPARATION TIME: 15 minutes

COOKING TIME: 25–30 minutes

PER SERVING: 220cals, 7g fat, 37g carbohydrate

SERVES 4

50g (2oz) ready-to-eat dried apricots, roughly chopped

50g (2oz) ground almonds

50g (2oz) raisins

50g (2oz) golden caster sugar

1 large egg white

2 large ripe pears, halved lengthways and core removed

Greek yogurt and a little warm honey for drizzling
   (optional)

A lovely dish for the autumn, but full of summer flavours.

1 Preheat the oven to 180°C (160°C fan oven) mark 4. Put the apricots in a small bowl with the almonds, raisins and sugar. Add the egg white and mix well.

2 Pile the almond mixture into the centre of the pears.

3 Put the pears in an ovenproof dish, transfer to the oven and bake for 25–30 minutes or until soft. Serve immediately with a spoonful of Greek yogurt drizzled with honey, if you like.

TO PREPARE AHEAD Complete the recipe to the end of step 1 up to one day in advance.

TO USE Complete the recipe.

Lime fruits

PREPARATION TIME: 6 minutes

COOKING TIME: 5 minutes

PER SERVING: 120cals, 0g fat, 31g carbohydrate

SERVES 4

Zest and juice of 4 limes – about 150ml (¼ pint)

3 level tbsp golden caster sugar

6 pieces of tropical fruit, such as papaya, melon or
   mango, peeled and sliced

Refreshing and tangy, this is the perfect pudding for anyone watching their weight. *Illustrated*

1 Heat the lime juice in a small pan with the sugar. Bring to the boil and allow to bubble for about 2–3 minutes or until all the sugar has dissolved.

2 Just before serving, add the lime zest to the warm syrup. Arrange the tropical fruits on serving plates and spoon over the lime syrup. Serve immediately.

Bananas grilled with cardamom butter

PREPARATION TIME: 5 minutes

COOKING TIME: 5 minutes

PER SERVING: 220cals, 11g fat, 32g carbohydrate

SERVES 4

2 green cardamom pods, split

50g (2oz) butter

50g (2oz) light muscovado sugar

4 bananas, unpeeled, slit along their length

Vanilla ice cream to serve

Cardamom pods contain the tiny seeds that give this butter its spicy-sweet flavour.

1 Beat the seeds of the cardamom pods into the butter and sugar.
2 Preheat the grill. Open out the bananas a little and put on a grill pan. Spoon a little of the flavoured butter into each one. Grill for 3–5 minutes, basting with the butter, until the bananas are soft and beginning to caramelise.
3 Serve the bananas piping hot with a little of the buttery sauce and some vanilla ice cream.

Hot fudge pears

PREPARATION TIME: 5 minutes

COOKING TIME: 15 minutes

PER SERVING: 320cals, 16g fat, 46g carbohydrate

SERVES 4

75g (3oz) butter

1tbsp golden syrup

75g (3oz) light muscovado sugar

4tbsp evaporated milk or single or double cream

4 pears, cored, sliced and chilled

Plain frozen yogurt or ice cream go well with these wickedly sweet fudge pears.

1 Melt the butter, syrup, sugar and evaporated milk together over a very low heat.
2 Stir thoroughly until all the sugar has dissolved completely, then bring the fudge mixture to the boil without any further stirring, and pour over the pears. Serve immediately.

Crumbly apple and cheese cake

PREPARATION TIME: 20 minutes

COOKING TIME: 50 minutes–1 hour plus 10 minutes cooling

PER SERVING: 330cals, 19g fat, 32g carbohydrate

MAKES 10 SLICES

90ml (3fl oz) sunflower oil plus extra to grease

175g (6oz) self-raising white flour

1 level tbsp baking powder

75g (3oz) light muscovado sugar

50g (2oz) raisins

50g (2oz) sultanas

50g (2oz) Brazil nuts, roughly chopped

550g (1¼lb) dessert apples, peeled, cored and thinly sliced

2 large eggs

225g (8oz) Caerphilly or Wensleydale cheese

Golden icing sugar to dust

This cake is full of good things – raisins, sultanas, nuts and apples, all combined with tangy cheese.

1 Preheat the oven to 180°C (160°C fan oven) mark 4. Grease and base-line a 5cm (2in) deep, 23cm (9in) round loose-bottomed flan tin.

2 Sift the flour and baking powder into a bowl. Stir in the sugar, raisins, sultanas, nuts and apples, and mix until combined. Beat the eggs with the oil and add to the dry ingredients. Stir until evenly incorporated.

3 Turn half the mixture into the prepared cake tin and level the surface. Crumble the cheese over the surface, then spoon on the remaining cake mix. Spread it to the edges of the tin, but do not smooth.

4 Bake for 50 minutes–1 hour or until golden and just firm.

5 Leave to cool in the tin for 10 minutes, then transfer to a wire rack. Serve warm, dusted with icing sugar.

Golden orange shortcake

PREPARATION TIME: 5 minutes

COOKING TIME: 10 minutes

PER SERVING: 510cals, 23g fat, 78g carbohydrate

SERVES 4

4 or 6 wedges of shortbread, depending on size

1 or 2 kumquats, sliced

6 oranges and clementines, peeled and segmented over a bowl, juice kept to one side

175g (6oz) golden caster sugar

75g (3oz) butter

Fresh orange juice

Cape gooseberries to serve

Kumquats and Cape gooseberries bring an exotic touch to this tasty dessert.

1 Put 1 or 2 wedges of shortbread on each serving plate and arrange the fruit on top.

2 Melt the caster sugar and the butter in a pan over a low heat, without stirring, until the sugar has dissolved. Bubble for 2–3 minutes or until golden caramel. Leave the pan on the heat.

3 Make up the reserved juice to 150ml (¼ pint) with fresh orange juice. Add to the pan and stir for 2 minutes. Pour over the shortbread and decorate with the Cape gooseberries.

Foil-baked figs with honey and marsala

PREPARATION TIME: 10 minutes
COOKING TIME: 13–18 minutes
PER SERVING: 140cals, 3g fat, 24g carbohydrate

SERVES 6

12 large ripe figs
Melted butter, to brush
1 cinnamon stick, roughly broken
6tbsp runny Greek honey
6tbsp marsala
Crème fraîche to serve

This is a good dish to make for a barbecue, when the coals have still got heat in them after the main course. It works just as well with plums or peaches but, depending on size, they'll need an extra 5–10 minutes on the barbecue.

1 Make a small slit in each fig, three-quarters of the way through. Take two sheets of foil big enough to hold the figs in one layer. With the shiny side uppermost, lay one piece on top of the other and brush the top piece all over with the melted butter.

2 Stand the figs in the middle of the foil and scatter over the broken cinnamon stick. Bring the sides of the foil together loosely, leaving a gap at the top, and pour in the runny honey and marsala. Finally, scrunch the edges of the foil together so that the figs are loosely enclosed.

3 Put the foil parcel on the barbecue and cook over medium hot coals for about 10–15 minutes, depending on how ripe the figs are, until very tender.

4 Just before serving, open up the foil slightly at the top and barbecue for a further 2–3 minutes to allow the juices to reduce and become syrupy.

5 Serve the figs immediately with a large dollop of crème fraîche and the syrupy juices spooned over.

Impress-your-friends apple tart

PREPARATION TIME: 15 minutes
COOKING TIME: 20–25 minutes
PER SERVING: 210cals, 11g fat, 25g carbohydrate

SERVES 8

375g packet ready-rolled puff pastry
500g (1lb 2oz) Cox's apples
Juice of 1 lemon
Golden icing sugar to dust

This apple tart couldn't be simpler to make, but it looks and tastes so good that it's bound to have everyone coming back for second helpings.

1 Preheat the oven to 200°C (180°C fan oven) mark 6. Put the pastry on a 28x38cm (11x15in) baking sheet and roll over lightly with a rolling pin to smooth down the pastry. Score lightly around the edge, to create a 3cm (1¼in) border.

2 Core and thinly slice the apples (don't peel them), then toss them in the lemon juice.

3 Carefully arrange the apple slices on top of the pastry, within the border. Turn the edge of the pastry halfway over, so that it reaches the edge of the apples, then press down and use your fingers to crimp the edge. Dust heavily with icing sugar.

4 Bake for 20–25 minutes until the pastry is cooked and the sugar has caramelised. Serve warm, dusted with more icing sugar.

INDEX